D0291938

"Dearest Amanda . . ."
An
Executive's
Advice to Her
Daughter

"Dearest Amanda . . ."
An
Executive's
Advice to Her
Daughter

Eliza G. C. *Collins*

1817
HARPER & ROW, PUBLISHERS, New York
Cambridge, Philadelphia, San Francisco, London
Mexico City, São Paulo, Singapore, Sydney

Portions of this work originally appeared in *Working Woman* magazine.

Designer: C. Linda Dingler

Library of Congress Cataloging in Publication Data

Collins, Eliza G. C.
    "Dearest Amanda . . .": an executive's advice to her daughter.

    1. Women in business.   2. Women executives.   I. Title.
HD6057.9.C65   1984   658.4′09′088042   83-48785
ISBN 0-06-015288-5

    85 86 87 88 10 9 8 7 6 5 4 3 2

This book is for Adam

"Dearest Amanda . . ."
An
Executive's
Advice to Her
Daughter

"Dearest Amanda . . .": *An Executive's Advice to Her Daughter* accurately portrays business behavior. However, to protect the privacy of individuals, the names used in this book are fictitious. The descriptions of individual traits and the locations of certain events have also been changed.

Dearest Amanda,

Your letter arrived this morning amid the usual clutter that descends on my desk. Sometimes I think the Fairmont mailroom has my station pegged as a dead-letter drop. I can scribble a response on most of the mail and Peggy makes a well-crafted and intelligent reply out of my scrawls. She is really me and I am her, as I've said to you many times. She tells me who I'm seeing when, what I think about a meeting I'm having in the afternoon, and what I am going to have for dinner. I think the only reason she sits at her desk out there and I sit at mine in here is a question of taste and imagination. She could never see herself sitting in this decorated palace I've constructed.

Of course I liked your roommate Ginny. She has the invaluable quality of making you think you are the only important person in the world while she speaks to you. It's captivating, though I do wonder whether she keeps enough in reserve to charm herself. Too much reaching out can mean too little taking in, the end result of which is a constant seeking of approval from others. Remember your fairy tales? It's always the wicked witches who check mirrors

1

on the wall. I am not, repeat not, saying Ginny is a wicked witch in embryo, but merely that mirrors, untrustworthy ones, are everywhere.

That sounds a little glib, but I swear, for me at least, the great struggle of life is knowing who and what you are in your own terms, defined by your own needs, not by someone else's. To get rewards from the world, we need rewards from ourselves first. To love others we need first to love ourselves. To go out in the world successfully, we need first to go inside ourselves.

I'm not sure why this seems important to me now, but it does. Maybe it's that you're out there now with all those years of superb education behind you and I am so painfully aware—it makes me hold my breath—that none of it can provide you with the tools you'll really need at Crandall Inc.—or at any place of work, for that matter.

Success comes from being able to handle the intricate and complex human relationships that make up a work-place community. After a certain point, your functional skills will count less and less. What will matter is how you treat other people, how other people see you, how you handle the disappointments that are inevitable, how you balance the conflicts that arise, how you hold a course you see as right when others disagree, and being right, whether you can feel worthy of success and can accept it as your own. And this crucial human element of business can't be taught, but must be learned. The key to it is a clear sense of your own self-worth. Don't ever doubt it—it's the one true guide you'll need and it can't fail you. The rest is child's play in comparison.

That said, Crandall's training program sounds like a

good one, though it's not surprising that you have the jitters and feel a bit in awe. If you get really anxious, why not try talking to your supervisor? From what you said, he sounds like a man who can understand some of what you're going through. Give him a try—it's one way to find out.

I have to go to a meeting in a minute. Peggy just poked her head in the door and gave me one of her you're-dawdling-when-you-ought-to-be-working looks, which keep me honest. So I must go. One last word, though. About the mirrors. We tend to see in them what we want. It's only when we don't question what we want that we stop looking.

Much love,
Mother

Dearest Amanda,

Once more unto the breach, dear daughter. I'm not really surprised by the reception you got when you confided to your supervisor about how anxious you become, and his reaction was—in a phrase—what's all the fuss about? I'm a dunce for suggesting you confide in him. Even the most ardent male supporters of women don't know what it's like to be one. Study after study has shown how impossible it is, for instance, for whites to understand blacks, to picture the experience. It is just as impossible for men to internalize the experience of women. Imagine trying to live without knowing the difference between intimacy and distance. I don't think women have any difficulty differentiating the two; it's natural. But what's even worse, men simply can't understand how isolated women are and how little notion we have of how to do things. We have had no one to copy.

After we moved to Chicago and I went back to work (you were five), I took a marketing position here. As you can imagine, Fairmont Corporation, then the world's leading manufacturer of small hand tools, wasn't populated by very many women. Six of us were scattered around in various departments like petunias in a gray field.

After a year or two of really hard work (I meant to stay and become a threat, if that's what it took), I went to a company-sponsored management development retreat which stands out in my memory not because of the communication skills it taught me, but because one of the leaders was a woman. Her name was Freda Morton. I filed into the large lecture hall with all the other attendees and got a seat near the rear. Then I stood up and leaned against the back wall so that I could see better.

Her topic was support groups at work, and if I remember correctly she didn't even touch on the male/female issue, there not being one at the time. She focused her remarks instead on the simple truths of candor and trust among employees and managers as a prerequisite for getting the most from the work force. I was happily listening to what seemed obvious to me, when the oddest thing happened. I started to cry. I was full of admiration and grief, and I was crying because I had seen what I had never had and wanted so much.

When you are alone, going into surgery, say, you don't have much time to think about being lonely. All your energies are spent in toughing it out, getting through the surgery, trusting to whatever health you have left to pull you through. But later, when you hear a voice saying the comforting things you tried to say to yourself, you can afford to realize how very alone you were. I stood there at the back of the hall watching this competent blond woman stride around the stage in front of a large group of men, saying simple obvious things, and I just wept. She was a confirming presence, while I was so alone most of the time.

As I checked around to see if anyone had noticed my crying, I observed bored tolerance on the faces of most of the men in the group. I'm sure many of them agreed with what Freda Morton was saying, but the process of her speaking had a different message for them. Afterward, I asked a friend of mine, Hal Davis, what he thought of that session, and he said, "Oh, it was all right, but I'm a little old to be mothered like that." What an enormous gulf there was between Hal and myself, and to varying degrees with other men too. And it still exists. Still!

What men don't understand is that most women grew up with passive mothers who didn't volunteer much guidance about anything except how to make beds, babies and bread, and say "I do." These skills are useless in business and most of us who have realized any success have done so feeling frightened and alone, without guides, without an internal sense of what is the right way. All the handbooks address the outward trappings of "making it," when what we need is a voice in our own heads, saying, "This way."

Men, on the other hand, have grown up hearing the voice that will be theirs as the voice of authority. I suppose that to Hal Davis, hearing Freda Morton speak was a nasty throwback to the kitchen, a place he'd escaped from years ago. While I, never having internalized a strong female voice, was as parched for it as the desert for rain.

Amanda, let me help, however I can. It's near impossible to become what we have no experience of, impossible to dream it, for we lack the images and words. I'd like you to have mine. What a breach to leap! Thanks for opening my eyes.

Can't wait to see you next weekend.

Much love,
Mother

April 14

Dearest Amanda,

I've hung the photograph in the living room right where I can see it. I still can't believe you had someone take it. Thank you so much. Oh, that house—I loved it so much, and I never thought I'd see it again. Your father and I had such a good time there.

I'm just back from the board meeting in Los Angeles. I think that Gerald is finally getting the idea that being CEO doesn't mean knowing everything himself. Over the years, I've had to dazzle him with "Delphi techniques" and "least-squares regression" before I could begin the harder job of delivering good straight simple marketing talk.

I saw your Aunt Sally, in fact spent an evening with her and her new husband in Santa Monica. He's very rich, as well as nice, and Sally now has everything she's always wanted. He thinks he's the most fortunate man in the world to have found her, and she, of course, agrees. Hers is a case of real luck.

Luck. Your letter confuses me some. First, after all your doubts, you tell me that things at Crandall are going well and that you're enjoying it more. Then you say that the project you were working so hard on turned out okay, and that the presentation went well. But after this lovely list of delights, you end it all by saying, "Of course, it was just luck."

It seems to me that ascribing success to luck is an excuse of the most deceptive sort. It says, This is not really me out here you're seeing, folks, this is old Lady Luck. It downplays your worth and says, "I'm really a failure." And you know how I feel about that!

There's a puzzle here. I always thought luck was finding a ten-dollar bill lying within grasp when you're a week away from payday. At Barnard, a bunch of us for whom stony broke was a way of life used to raid the beau parlors at night. Those were small chapel-like rooms off the main college lounge, equipped with a small couch and two chairs, where young ladies could entertain young men before the great gong went off at ten-thirty each evening. Sometime around ten-thirty-five, we would sneak down and, sweeping through the beau parlors, garner the change that had slipped out of amorous males' pockets as they

7

performed their allowed calisthenics on the couches. We netted about three or four dollars a night, which would be the next day's cups of coffee and English muffins at the Chock Full o' Nuts down the street. Finding the money on the street would have been luck. Finding it in the couches was industry, something very different.

When I first went to work for Howard Industries, I shared an office and an apartment with another management trainee, Susan Donovan. Susan had gone to Smith and graduated magna cum laude. She was one of those girls who did everything with a sort of effortless grace. You know the kind. Susan would spend the night before a report was due working for maybe an hour, then she'd go out for the evening and come home exhausted and decide to get up early in the morning for a last look at the data. I didn't hate Susan Donovan when she turned in a report to our VP after partying the night away; I just never understood why she did it, let alone how.

One night we went to a poker party together. I wasn't a bad player—I could keep track of the cards reasonably well and won a little more than I lost. Susan, it turned out, was a terrible player. And that night I learned about both Susan and luck. One hand we played, there were six of us and the game was seven-card stud. Susan had the worst possible hand showing and could win only if God dealt the last card down and was on her side. I had the thing sewed up and knew it. When it came time to declare, there were no surprises. Two of the players (two had folded) went low and Susan and I went high. She won, I lost. I was dumbfounded. Anyone could see that she should have folded on a previous round.

"Why didn't you fold?" I asked.

"I'd rather play than watch," she said. "Besides, I like being lucky."

I couldn't understand it. But then, years later, I did. Susan didn't want to win by trying to. If she won through luck, she could always fail with grace and she wouldn't have to take failure seriously. This attitude rules out success.

With a game of poker, the outcome doesn't matter one way or the other unless you're betting your paycheck. In other things, real things, like examinations and writing reports and getting them done on time, it does matter, and the habit of luck can be fatal. Susan's reports were on time but they lacked effort. What I couldn't understand about Susan is why she didn't want to try for success. She had everything going for her—boundless energy and brains.

The year I lived with Susan, things went on pretty much as I've described until we underwent our performance appraisals at work. Suddenly, I learned I was to be transferred to a coveted line job in the marketing department, while Susan was assigned as a staff assistant to the vice-president of personnel, in those days a place of no return.

At dinner, Susan was subdued. I kept repeating inanities like "It isn't fair" and "You should go talk to Sam Cohen" (our VP). Finally, when she still hadn't said much but had gloomed over her steak, I heard myself utter the self-denigrating and apologetic phrase, "I only got that job through luck." I was so afraid that Susan wouldn't like me anymore because I was going away, somewhere she couldn't go. I thought I'd have to leave her behind, and I didn't want her to think it was intentional.

9

She looked at me and smiled, then she touched my hand and said something I'll never forget: "You can always phone, you know. It's not like you're dying."

Winning is a little like dying, because you do leave people behind. In a road race that's very obvious; some are left panting or spinning their wheels at the starting line. And I suppose we feel that, like dying, winning is final. But Susan was right. Winning didn't mean I'd lose her. Nor does trusting to brains, not luck, mean going away.

I still hear from Susan. She's married to an Englishman and spends most of her time flying from London to Paris, buying women's fashions for a chic little shop she owns in Mayfair. Susan was never cut out for the corporate life and maybe her holding back had more sense to it than we knew at the time. Winning means different things for different people, thank God.

Give my best to Ginny. And Tom. Tom who?

Feel free to reverse the charges.

Much love,
Mother

September 20

Dearest Amanda,

Here's something that will amuse you. I went to a dinner party last night and was seated next to a Hungarian count. Can you believe that they still exist? They do, and they still come with monocles and with ribbons on their broad tuxedoed chests. Count Marchansky didn't actually fight in any battles—I think he sat out WWII in London in his sister's flat, surrounded by warring servants—but nonetheless he had ribbons. I inquired about them and found that they were bestowed by different international institutions for his charitable works and efforts on behalf of refugees. They looked as splendid as he did, with his large head and his mass of thick white hair. He had dark eyebrows and a very prominent nose and full lips that smiled easily.

Although he paid attention to Nancy Lowe, who sat on his other side, he was very attentive to me, complimenting me at every turn, not only for my dress and hair but also for my remarks, which, he said, were at once witty and penetrating.

I hadn't felt so bewitching in a long time and figured that something must have happened to me without my realizing it. Maybe it's because I've lost a few pounds, I thought, that I have become so suddenly alluring, or maybe, all my experience to the contrary, spending hours having my face done yesterday morning really did make a difference.

At one point during the dinner, Count Marchansky turned away from Nancy and said to me in a whisper that at last an American woman had dispelled all his doubts that we were finally a civilized country and one he'd have to think about visiting more often—if, of course, I was going to be willing to accept his invitations to dinner, the opera, the occasional drive in the country. I, as they say in the regency romances, demurred and smiled shyly.

After dinner, the guests milled about, making small

talk before leaving. I strolled to the library with Dottie Soloman, my hostess, to see her new art acquisition. (It's an Andersen portrait and very nice.) As we passed the door to the sitting room, I overheard a familiar voice telling some unseen figure that she at last had convinced the speaker of our country's civilization and so forth. Dottie laughed and said that the Count was going to have his hands full. I, suddenly relieved to find myself me after all, and not the product of some magician's brew, suggested that he be given another ribbon to adorn his chest, signifying his labors on behalf of American divorcees. "It might," said Dottie, taking my arm, "alert the unwary."

For one minute there, maybe even for an hour, I had believed the poseur and not myself. This is not to say that I didn't look perfectly fine and that I wasn't clever and insightful; it's only that for a time I had relinquished my assessment of him—for he was clearly a flatterer—for his approval of me.

I wonder if you might be going through the same sort of experience with the job offer you've had, are about to accept, but feel uneasy about. Is the issue how you say "no"?

That makes sense to me. Do you remember when you and Sylvia Grimes were best friends? You used to play together every afternoon after school. Most of the time, I remember, you spent trying to sneak into other people's gardens and pretending they were yours. Your favorite belonged to Mrs. Montefiore. She had a greenhouse and in the wintertime you would sneak through the back gate and saunter along the greenhouse pathways, sniffing flowers and on occasion picking a few to put in your hair. I know all this because Mrs. Montefiore told me that one of the delights of her old age was watching the two of you from her sickbed, as you enjoyed what she had long been unable to take pleasure from.

One day you came home in a fit of rage from one of your afternoons out playing princesses in the garden. You jumped up and down in one spot while you told me about it. Apparently Sylvia had told you she couldn't play that afternoon, so you had gone to Mrs. Montefiore's yourself for a solitary stroll through your fantasy. You entered the greenhouse and found Sylvia there with another schoolmate. Rather than show Sylvia how hurt you were, you pretended to be glad to see her, and spent the rest of the day in forced jollity, trying to include Phyllis in the special place that had been yours and Sylvia's. You even asked them to dinner. You were filled with deep fury and unhappiness, but somehow your dislike of Sylvia at that moment got turned into supreme politeness, as if your anger was unallowable.

The same thing happened to me with my Count. I didn't really like him and thought his attentions unctuous and insincere. But somehow it seemed inappropriate to not like him actively, so I slipped back into the easier stance of accepting gracefully his fawning overtures.

Do you feel you have to take the job because it's been offered to you? My guess is that you somehow think that if you say, "No, thanks," there must be something wrong with you, not the job. Otherwise, why is it so hard to turn it down?

Give yourself time to work out what would please you. Do you want to leave Crandall? It's important to develop your own idea of yourself so that you won't get your head turned for even a moment by the Hungarian counts who will try to recruit you. If you have an idea of what you want, you can hold it up against their ideas to see if there's a fit. Take your time; you've earned it.

And finally, no, I'm not ducking the issue about you and Tom. Of course you don't have to have separate bedrooms when you come next weekend. Now that I've said it, and know it's the right answer, I wonder why it was so hard for you to ask and for me to reply. What is it that binds mothers and daughters in so tight a grapple, like fighters in a mutual time-out?

Much love,
Mother

P.S. Also consider the risks of job-hopping too soon. It's important to build a good track record.

November 18

Dearest Amanda,

I hope you weren't worried when you called the office yesterday and Peggy told you I had gone to the hospital. She said you believed her when she reported that I was all right, just a little dopey from a bump on the head. That should have been reassuring; Peggy doesn't kid around when it comes to my noggin.

Maybe this adventure has knocked some sense into

me. I was running down the driveway with my arms full of garbage bags to catch the trashman. Thinking how efficient it was of me to get rid of the garbage on the right day—as if a few trash bags in the can would make the coming week simply too untidy to bear—I felt my feet slip on an icy patch where the driveway takes a dip. I landed on my rear, but my head bounced back onto the ice. Fortunately, the garbageman saw me slip and came to help me up; otherwise I might have lain there quite a while, splayed amid dog food cans and kitty litter. By the time I got to work I had a towering headache and a swelling that Peggy insisted was getting bigger even as she touched it. To appease her, I went off to the hospital and they kept me for the night, I suppose wanting to watch the bump grow too. Well, I disappointed them and have nothing to show for my fall but a stiff neck and a messy driveway.

What happened was quite simple and rather predictable when you consider that I'm always trying to do too many things at the same time, too fast. I picked up the habit from your grandfather, who, when pressed to go to church, used to cover the donation envelope with a list of things he had to do later in the day. That way, he said, he could live two lives, cramming as much as possible into one so he could enjoy the other. The only problem was that he was always living the first of his two lives. The day he died, he had a pocketful of bits of paper covered with crossed-off items. Finding them, your grandmother said with unrestrained and healthy bitterness that "he'd probably run out of excuses not to have a good time and resorted to the big one." After that she was able to cry.

I did have time in the hospital, though, to stop and

wonder what all the rushing was about. And I remembered your writing that your life has become a battleground where obligations and appointments war with each other for your time. You said you've even resorted to lists and an answering machine so that you won't miss calls from people requesting more of your time. It's wonderful to be efficient and I'm sure your training period at Crandall will be a success on account of it, but I think there's an important difference between conscientiously attending to the jobs we do and the feeling of burden that sometimes accompanies them, which is what makes us sweat and heave with frustration while we carry them out.

I must have told you about the day the basement filled with water. It was a summer Saturday and your father was away on a business trip. You were at Sylvia's, and I had the day to myself, a rarity and a gift, or so it seemed. First I would tackle the things that were really necessary, like doing some laundry and shopping, and paying a few bills, then I was going to take myself, a book I'd been meaning to read, a sandwich and a bottle of beer to the beach and get gorgeously tanned for when your father came home. The image of my afternoon glowed in the back of my head while I did my errands in the morning.

When I got home, I went down to the basement to transfer clothes from the washer to the dryer. As soon as I opened the door, I knew something was wrong. The basement was a pool, with the level still rising. Facing the greasy wet enemy that was stealing my day from me, I thought: I have to clean it. But I didn't want to do it. I so wanted my afternoon that I had worked hard for and deserved.

With a great deal of sighing and groaning, I set to with mops and buckets and shovels. There was a *lot* of water. When I realized I'd never get to the beach and had at least another hour of bailing to do, I flung the bucket at the wall and screamed. I shouted at your father that I hated him for leaving me with this thankless job. Then I heard myself cry out, "You don't love me and you never did." Of course, nobody answered. Nobody was there, actively not loving me. Wet and sticky and dirty, I was completely alone.

But because I had to do an onerous job, it felt as if someone was saying that I deserved the mop-bucket life. It's easy to attribute such sentiments to others when they are around and when they carelessly, as all of us do at times, don't notice that we're working our butts off. But when there was no one there, it became only too obvious that the slave girl feeling was mine and mine alone.

You mentioned that you wished your boss would take more notice of what you do and of how hard you work, of how many nights you stay late after everyone else has gone home. I can't help wondering if you're mopping up the basement and seeing the work as significant of something more than performing a job. We work for the unseen at every turn, and hate it when it makes us work too hard for too little reward. In thinking we're working for others, we forget that we can work for ourselves. I can't stress enough how debilitating working to please others is.

Thinking back to that day in the basement, I understand what was wrong with it from the start. What I had wanted, remember, was time to get to the beach. Part of that desire for time was for myself—the book, the beer, the afternoon off. A big part of it, though, was for pleasing your father. But "time" is an empty idea, it's not a thing to desire for itself. The issue is not the lack of time but how we feel about ourselves and who we're spending time for. The question is who we perceive is in control. When you feel as if you're working for yourself, exemplifying some image you have of what you want to be, a hectic day is a high. On such days, time is all on your side. When you're working for someone else, it's slavery and time becomes an enemy. Your poor father—I used to give him such a hard time when he didn't appreciate how "pressed for time" I was, or my sacrifices.

When you work late at night or rush from one appointment to another, cursing friends and colleagues who make these demands on you, who are you doing it for? If for them, that way lies fury that makes some of us quit altogether, some bleat at the unfairness of it all, and others shoulder their burdens quietly, screaming silently to themselves all the while.

I know it may sound like the ultimate in corporate heresy, but *try seeing your job as something you own.* In that way you can control the time and energy it takes to do it. Believe me, it's amazing how much more you can have of both. It's even possible—impossible dream though it may seem—to enjoy mopping up.

I don't think I'm going to clean the driveway when I get home. I had thought of it, but my neck is still stiff and the mess can wait another day. Better yet, I'll pay Jimmy Rogers to do it. He's always looking for extra jobs, for the right reasons. He gets paid for them. Me, I think I'll take a long soak and flop into bed with a good book and a beer.

It's at times like this that I miss the good days with your father. There's much I'd like to tell him, now in the dying time of the year when the desire to be tanned is fruitless and I want no escapes from the second life I try to lead.

Much love,
Mother

P.S. Is Tom coming for Thanksgiving? Millie is dying to see you. She's determined to do sweet potatoes and marshmallows, so be prepared!

February 3

Dearest Amanda,

I just got back from San Francisco, where I'd been to attend a Makepiece board meeting. Makepiece has become a large, sprawling company, doing about $3.5 billion in operating revenues this year. With all its rubber products, it's trying valiantly to shift the main product line from tires to more industrial goods, such as roofing material, industrial hoses, and so forth. It's been pretty successful at this transition, though it suffers simultaneous growth and death pains. Part of the business is so mature that things grow like asparagus; and for newer divisions, it's changing diapers all the time.

When I first joined the board, I knew nothing about the business and kept my mouth shut most of the time. But as time passed and the intricacies of the balance sheet and even some of the technological processes became more familiar, so did I. I enjoy the meetings a great deal. Partly, it's the ritual I like. The night before, we usually have a dinner, splendid affairs at which we glitter. Being the only woman, I get an undue amount of attention, which both flatters and annoys me. It was ever thus. At the dinners, we exchange the social talk that makes the business world tick. We pick each other's brains about problems we all share—dealing with foreign competition, the labor market, unions. But we also get to know each other in a more personal way. You know, most of the people on the board hold supremely responsible positions and have few if any people in their own companies to share problems with. Our gathering is not group therapy, but it gives everyone a sense that other people are concerned with the same fundamental problems. And they are, believe me!

Before the meeting itself we meet for a glass of sherry, and then we troop into the boardroom and sit ourselves at our assigned places around an enormous Honduran mahogany table.

The dynamics of these meetings fascinate me. As soon as we sit down, the roles shift. We are no longer independent people, but a group with a leader. We each slip into this new role in our own way. I find I twiddle my pencil on my pad; it gives me something to do over which I have control. Others rearrange papers. We become quite dignified as we listen to reports from the various committees and to Makepiece personnel making presentations. I worry at times that we are too formal.

Makepiece's chairman, Bill Rawlings, has asserted that he values our individual contributions and competencies, but sometimes, when it comes to expressing ourselves, even the most relaxed and experienced (Albert Epping, Makepiece's investment banker, and Sam Rubenstein, CEO of Finley, the steel construction manufacturer, are the best) hem and haw until Rawlings has made some indication of how he'd like things to go.

Recently, because of all the changes Makepiece has been going through, some sticky issues have been coming up, and at these times it bothers me that our expertise comes down to reading Rawlings' various nods and facial expressions. During this meeting, for instance, we were presented with the figures on a factory in rural Tennessee that has been losing money for a while, even though the quality of the work has been high and the employees diligent and productive. The problem is that the product is part of a declining industry and there's no way to resuscitate it. The figures and the prognosis both indicate that the factory has to be shut down. Of course, it's in the company's interest to keep the plant operating at top efficiency as long as it can. The question is, how soon do we tell the employees that they're out of a job if we wish to maintain a full work force to the end?

I feel strongly that the employees ought to be told as soon as a decision is made. We owe them time to resettle, retrain, and so forth. Their loyalty is high and if we treat them well, I think we can expect the same in return. Rawlings understood my point of view, but he wants to delay informing them until the factory has completed some fairly substantial orders. It's a judgment call, and after I made my point I left it and didn't argue it further. I don't know how Rawlings will decide; we don't get involved in

21

the implementation of decisions like this. I left the meeting convinced that Rawlings' way was wrong, but at the same time I wanted him to be right. For a moment, I thought that it might have been inappropriate of me to argue as I had, even that my attitude might be wrong. (You can guess how much I like feeling that!)

In one of your letters you expressed the fear that you don't have any closely held values, that you're a vacillating wimp of a person because you find yourself nodding in agreement to whatever your boss says without even listening very hard to him. This you said happens even when you discuss nonbusiness matters—like books. He liked Rawls' *Theory of Justice,* and you chimed in that it was wonderful when you hadn't even halfway finished it (I didn't either).

My "life in sports" has always provided parallels to my business quandaries. One summer I played a lot of tennis. I decided to enter the Matunuck tennis tournament, and found myself in the semifinals against Marianne Smith, a polished player.

The first set went surprisingly quickly and I won it. Marianne was coasting around, seemingly convinced that she had the match wrapped up. She woke up during the second set and won it 6–4, but I was still respectable. The third set was a real test. I was playing out of some inner tennis manual that I didn't know I'd read. We reached 4–all and it was Marianne's serve. I knew that if I took her serve I might win. I had lost mine only once in the second set and the odds were I could do it. My game was flawless. I rushed the net, putting away her returns of my return of service before she even knew what I was up to (a little technique borrowed from basketball). I won the game on my first advantage.

In the last game I was ahead 30–15, when Marianne lobbed a ball over my head and I ran back for it. Keeping my eye on the ball, I tripped over the backline tape where a staple had come out, and flew through the air, landing on my right elbow. When I stood, I couldn't straighten out my arm. People rushed onto the court to see if I was all right, and Marianne came around from the other side, full of decent remorse. She didn't want to win that way. I was on the verge of tears from pain and frustration, but at the same time I was aware that in one small creepy crawly part of my mind I felt the most absurd feeling of all—relief. Not that I hadn't won, but that Marianne hadn't lost.

On most issues you can divide the world into two classes of people. Some have messy drawers and clean surfaces while others have messy surfaces and neat drawers. Around the issue of tennis or the boardroom or you in conversation with your boss, the division is between those who root for the underdog and those who can't, even when it is themselves.

I've often wondered about that feeling of relief that I hadn't beaten Marianne as I think I could have. At the time, it would have seemed unnatural. Marianne had always been better than I, and I had the idea that only one person could be at the top of the heap. If it had been me, I'd have lost my bearings. My position, or so I thought, was somewhere near the top, but not the top. *She* was supposed to win.

We all want our leaders and mentors to be right and smart. If they aren't, we're all in danger, especially when they're in powerful positions. And so it might seem a little risky to find out that they're not perfect. In feeling powerless, some people are so afraid of the top dogs that they try to tear them down. Others want to preserve them. Some people wanted Marianne to lose because she was the best around, and I wanted her to win for the same reason.

With our bosses, subordinacy sometimes turns into subservience, and we adopt their values as our own. We don't work as well that way, however. When subservience is so easy and so acceptable, how do you maintain your integrity? Keep your eye on your purpose. What I do when I find myself being supremely agreeable is to slow down. Before leaping in with the quick and easy response, I try to think about what I really want the outcome to be. Often just a moment's hesitation will serve. What is your goal? Is it to please your boss with flattery, pretending to like what he does, or is it to have an interchange? By offering your boss your true opinion, you give him something to work with, and you'll learn more about what he thinks. No one likes to play with someone who can't return the ball. If I'd beaten Marianne, I would not have deposed her permanently. We'd merely have had better games, more often.

What's wrong with always rooting for the person on top (or the underdog) is that in doing so we don't want a match fair and square, which is the only and the best way to run things. So cheer for the game, and forget the players.

Hooray for me! I just got a call from Bill Rawlings. What a nice and thoughtful man he really is, besides being handsome. (I didn't tell you *that* part. Maybe *that* explains some of my awe.) He called to say that he'd been thinking over what I said and just wanted me to know he'd decided to tell management in Tennessee to level with the employees from the start and to begin some in-house programs to help them at the same time. Now, if that's not the natural order of things, what is? I am so pleased.

Oh, damn, why did I have to break my elbow? I really did want to win that match!

Much love,
Mother

May 12

Dearheart,

Please find enclosed the birth certificate for one Amanda Hardy, born in Boston on March 10, 1954. They said you were the most beautiful baby in the hospital and they were right. Would you like the whole box? It's got all your report cards from school, envelopes of hair cut at various stages (when you were born it was black, isn't that amazing?), letters from your father and some from your paternal grandparents.

Do you ever hear from them now? I got over wanting to explain to them about the divorce long ago, but it would be so much easier for you if they could know what really happened. But if your father could never understand it, I suppose it's a lot to ask that they should. What a weird lot you drew. Oh, well, between us we produced you, so we can't be all bad.

I wish you'd known my parents. Do you remember visiting them in Providence? I suppose not, you were so small. My father adored you. You were the only one he'd stop his interminable chores for. He'd sit you on the grass and hand you the circular water sprayer, which you'd promptly put on your head. Then he'd turn it on, and you'd become a chortling water fountain. I don't think I ever saw him as happy as he was those afternoons with you.

Millie says hi. If you dropped her a line she'd put it in *her* memory box. Sometimes I wonder who really raised you.

Love,
Mom
XXXOOO

September 27

Dearest Amanda,

It's a wonderful idea for you to buy a condo. Why were you so hesitant to bring it up, and of course I'll be glad to help with the down payment. The only advice I'll give on buying is to check out the neighborhood for things that you might not be immediately interested in yourself, such as schools and parks. Those things are of prime interest to people you might sell to in the future, so should be of concern to you. The two bits of property you described both sound nice in their own ways, but I wonder why you lean toward the less expensive one on West Ninetieth that you like less. Sure it'll cost less to keep up, but you're going to make more money next year than this, and by your own admission you like the other one better. You say it's sunny and warm and you like the east side of town better; so where's the debate?

The more I think of it, the more I think there might be something in that attitude that's reflected in your story about your lunch with Peter Shell. Please forgive me if I sound too motherish—it *is* hard to give up the role completely—but when you wrote and described your interview with Shell I was completely baffled. When you started out talking about the lunch and how complimentary he was about the work you'd been doing for Crandall and how impressed he'd been, I could tell he was going to make you a job offer of some kind to bring you into his department. And it sounds as if he did, but you didn't hear it. He made an off-the-cuff remark about your participating on a trial basis in some projects he had and you wrote about it as if he were merely describing plans to you. Why would he do that if he didn't want to find out if you were interested? Executives like Peter Shell—as you describe him, anyway—aren't going to spend time telling trainees about projects unless there's a reason. It sounds as if it didn't occur to you that he could have been thinking about you for a position. Can't you imagine yourself as someone he would be interested in? Aren't you good enough? Believe me, I know how hard it is to keep feeling special every day.

One day last week, after Peggy had brought in the morning mail and the appointment book, and we'd gone through what we had to do, answered a few letters and made a few phone calls, she announced that I could take the afternoon off.

I said, "Peggy, you've got something up your sleeve. Empty it."

She said, "Margaret, it's simple—you're a mess."

Only Peggy could say those words and convey at the same time that she didn't mean I was falling apart before her eyes and had to check into the booby hatch. I took out a mirror I kept in my drawer and looked at my face. It was mine, without noticeable traces of food.

"What do you mean?" I said. "I'm fine."

"Of course you're fine," she said, "but you need an overhaul. I've seen that suit three times in the last two weeks, your hair is straggly at the ends, and you look gray."

I got up and looked in the floor-length mirror on the back of the closet door. There I was, all five foot eight and a half inches of me, a little lumpy, hair a sheenless unshaped brown mop on my head. She was right. I looked like hell. Oh, it was a fairish sort of hell and the dog wouldn't throw me out if the cat dragged me in, but she wouldn't lick me with any delight, either. Without letting me sit down, Peggy took out my coat, slung it around my shoulders, and told me to "'op it." She called ahead and got me an appointment with Sidney, who trimmed and pushed my hair around so that it's now perkier and highlighted. I spent the rest of the afternoon shopping. I didn't buy one suit. Instead I bought outfits and dresses. I was on a spree, but when the saleslady started wrapping them all up, I felt suddenly as if the fun part was over.

It reminded me of when every year my mother used to take me to buy a new pair of Mary Janes and she'd never let me wear them home. They would get wrapped carefully in that black-gray paper that was supposed to keep them shiny, and when we got home Mother would put them on the top shelf of my closet.

I wore my Mary Janes maybe ten times a year, at birthday parties and holidays. Then my feet would have grown and we'd go out the next year and repeat the whole mummifying process. My keenest wish was to wear my Mary Janes home from the store and every day. But my mother said the toes would become scuffed and then I wouldn't have anything special to wear when I needed it. She was right, of course, but another message was conveyed as well. That for the 355 days of the year that I didn't wear my Mary Janes, I wasn't special. And over the year, as I came to judge them for myself, the days when I was special grew fewer.

It was the same with the black leather handbag, the gloves and the gorgeous green skirt with turquoise stripes that my grandmother bought for me when I went off to college. Four years later, can you believe I had never used any of them? There never seemed to be a day special enough. I was saving them like my virginity, and like my virginity I tossed them away as if they hadn't been special at all.

If we can't conceive of ourselves in a certain way, we can't see it when other people treat us that way. During one part of my college time (when I wasn't wearing the skirt), I was infatuated with a young man who was considered to be not only "impossible," which meant he said lewd and clever things, but also "unreliable," which meant he'd take you out, try to get you to bed and, regardless, not call for over a week. He treated girls very casually. But he was extremely smart and attractive and had a vulnerable air that convinced all the girls who ever dated him that somewhere, somehow, he was a decent sort. I, of course, saw him as "impossible" and "unreliable," so that when we did start to date, on a regular off-and-on basis, I was sure that each time I saw him would be the last. Oh, I was cool about it, never letting on that it bothered me, while all the time I was iced anxiety.

One day we bumped into each other in the library and had a conversation as meaningful as "Hi, how are you." At least it seemed that way to me. I do remember that he mentioned a concert he was going to the next evening, but that was about all. The next night I sat at home in the dorm, fretting and fussing because I knew Sam was at the concert, I supposed with someone else. About ten o'clock, the phone rang and it was Sam. The concert was over and he wanted to know why I hadn't met him there. I was speechless. I finally admitted that I didn't know what he was talking about. He explained that when we met the day before, he'd asked me if I wanted to go to the concert. I, so convinced that my involvement with him was a passing thing and that I was nothing special, had simply not heard an invitation in what he'd said. I couldn't imagine myself as being someone Sam wanted to see regularly, which, without my noticing it, is what he had begun to do. He, it turned out, was far more involved in our relationship than I. I had spent so much energy protecting myself from disappointment, I didn't have any left for partaking in the fun while it was going on.

It's so much easier to be removed than it is to be

disappointed, it's not surprising that I didn't hear Sam's invitation. Of course, he could have been more precise about it, as Peter Shell could have been much more direct about his proposal to you. But other people are protecting themselves as well, strange as that may seem, and I'm sure Sam was just as frightened of my rejection as I was of not getting an invitation. After all, I was the one who had been so "unbothered" that it must have appeared that I really didn't care.

Do you suppose Peter Shell couched his probings in such vague terms because he was put off by your insouciance?

The only way out of this muddle is to fight the root problem: feeling unspecial. The other day when I was watching those lovely clothes being wrapped up, feeling as if they belonged to someone else, I struck a blow for being special every day. I asked the saleslady to unpack the blue dress with the black belt because I'd decided to wear it home. After I'd changed and she'd put my suit into the carry bag, I took a detour on the way out of the store. I stopped off at the children's shoe department to see if they carry Mary Janes. They do. Did you know they now make Mary Janes in red as well as black? Standing there, I was struck with the most intense desire to own one more pair of those shoes, although they don't make them in my size and I'd never wear them if they did. I look abysmal in flats, as you know. Also, I felt it was absurd and a little backward to buy a pair of Mary Janes for old times' sake, so I did the next best thing. I bought the most beautiful pair of patent-leather pumps I've ever seen. And I wore them home too.

Did you really want the black coat? I think it's still

31

in storage, but I can send it to you. Why not get a new one?

Much love,
Mother

P.S. Give my best to Ginny and tell her if she passes through Chicago on her drive to San Francisco and needs a place to lay over for a day, she's welcome. I'd love having her.

December 10

Dearest Amanda,

Herein one house present. Your place is beautiful. It's so sunny and you've decorated it magnificently. It makes me happy just thinking of you there. You don't know how important it is to me to know where you're sitting when you talk on the phone or write.

Anyway, here's a token I picked up in Japan, outside Kagoshima. Something to put your tea cozy on. I had a simply wonderful time there. What a country, and what a manufacturing paradise! The U.S. has a lot of catching up to do. Us too. Our visits are too rare, and too rare to be so rare. Can't wait to see you at Christmas.

Much love,
Mother

Dearest Amanda,

Now I understand why you can't join me in Jamaica. I suddenly figured it out. You hate warm water and glorious sun in mid-February. I must have raised you with all the virtues firmly in place—good, solid, hardworking attitudes that fortify you through harsh, horrible winters. I know, your love of shoveling got the better of you, or was it your fiendish attachment to freezing temperatures? Well, I confess to not feeling one ounce of remorse or contrition at missing them. When I'm working, I wonder if it will ever be possible to escape the daily frenzies, but miraculously, when I get away to a warm beach I succumb to the lovely myth that life can be a gift, for a bit at least. With the first swim in soft green water I know as surely as I've known anything what the priorities are—warmth, love, the pursuit of a conch on the crawl, a bit of shade to read in, and the perfect rum punch at five o'clock. And this transformation happens so quickly. Point of view is all.

When you called yesterday to say you couldn't come, you sounded so glum, I shouldn't tease. I'm well aware that my priorities are rum-soaked, but my hearing is still unimpaired. It seems a ticklish situation that you're in. Phil Daniels sounds like a man with a deep streak of penury and few resources. People who don't acknowledge others' contributions to projects populate all businesses and in the long run they lose out. Good people stop working hard for them or quit altogether. He's a problem for sure. But the real issue seems to be how you're dealing with being so angry at him.

What you described, all this conscientious extra work, sounds like revenge working to me. Revenge working suffices up to a point, but then all that buried fury will out, and the work will be the target. Oh, Lord, did I learn that lesson well. When I was at Howard, I worked on a project with a guy who was a compleat pettifogger. Not only did Matthew Kransky insist that I keep my desk as neat as he kept his—"a messy desk indicates a messy mind," he'd say—but he'd find something wrong in absolutely everything I did. If I drafted the perfect memo, he'd simply have to rewrite a few phrases to make it "just right," where the rephrasing was a matter of taste. I swallowed my fury every time this happened and resolved that the next little job I did would be perfect. Of course, it never was. The cycle we got into was pernicious. He'd criticize, I'd work harder, he'd criticize. Finally, overwrought and desperate, I simply struck out at the job itself.

One night, working late over a report that was due on our mutual superior's desk the next afternoon, gorged with loathing for Matthew Kransky and striking a blow for liberty, I simply didn't attend to what I was doing. At the time, of course, I thought I was ever sharp and precise, so I was filled with as much horror as Matthew when the report was presented to Bruce Mitchell. I'd done every graph in millions instead of thousands of dollars. Oh, the chagrin.

After the embarrassment faded and the incident was written off to overwork, which heaven knows was the case as well, I knew I'd have to take a new tack. I couldn't work any harder to catch my own sabotage than I was already working. Besides, my social life was in chaos. The problem was solved in this case by Matthew. He quit the next week, having received a better offer, and so I felt free to ask him what he thought of me and my work. What a twerp, but I'll never forget his comment. "Margaret," he said, "you worry too much and work too hard." He obviously thought more of the object of his nasty taunts than I had.

Seeing as it's not likely that your Phil Daniels will quit Crandall, maybe you'll have to work double time for a while to ensure that you don't slip wacky numbers into the reports you do for him. But that way is exhausting and so can't suffice for the long haul. Better to attack the problem head-on. By that I don't mean kicking his teeth in, though it's a thought that pleases. I wouldn't tell him he's a lousy manager either, or that you'd really like some recognition for your work. If he's like many I know, he'll see asking for recognition in an area that threatens him as a sign that you can't take the heat. Phil Daniels sounds like a man with no future and probably a past to protect as well. Assuming you want to stay in that job for a while to learn it (you say Daniels is reasonably good at what he does even though he's a pack rat with rewards), attack the problem from the inside. What grabs you so? (What grabbed me? What makes us feel so attacked?)

The serpent strikes even in paradise. Last night I

went to a cocktail party at one of the other houses that border the blue lagoon. I wore the green Indian dress you sent and gold sandals. The night air was my wrap. Content with my day and myself, I wasn't prepared for a snake named Louise Harper. I was talking with my host when this blond buzz saw appeared at his side. She took his arm and, hugging it like a loaf of French bread, exclaimed rapturously about the glorious night and the wonderful party. Then, looking at me (I'd met Louise years ago when we were both young mothers, me a working one, she a professional troublemaker), she said, "How'd you get here?" Although her question was not about my mode of transportation, I answered, "By foot. I'm next door." She swung her head in the direction of the house that looked like a sparkling gem reflected in the lagoon and said, "A bit over your head, isn't it?"

I wanted to punch Louise in the mouth on the spot and rip the bleached hair from her dried-up scalp. Instead I excused myself and did some fast revenge eating at the buffet table. With a full mouth and a stomach of bile, I tried to work out what had got to me. Do I care what Louise Harper thinks? I used to. She could make me feel terribly guilty about you when I was working and you were at home with Millie. In those days I resolved the issue with myself by determining that I would be a lousy mother to you all the time if I stayed home, rather than a passably good one most of the time if I worked.

The issue never was what Louise Harper thought; it was what you thought. And it still is. But even that doesn't settle the stomach and release tightened muscles. You know, I think a part of me interpreted your glumness as castigation (echoed by Louise Harper) that I shouldn't be down here enjoying myself while you were up there with something less palatable on your plate than what Millie offered in my absence. I don't know if you think that or not (knowing you, it's probably the last thought in your mind), but I responded to the bell.

What do you assume is in Daniels' mind when he doesn't reward you? Maybe you've been concentrating too hard on what he does and doesn't say and not enough on what you think of him.

What you think will always be important to me, but more crucial—and here the stomach relaxes—is what I think of myself. Phil Daniels, Matthew Kransky and Louise Harper are sad imitations of people. I'm doing just fine and so are you.

Tonight I plan on having a much better time. Remember my mentioning Bill Rawlings, CEO of Makepiece? He's anchored his boat near the lagoon and has invited me on board for dinner. I think I'll wear the green dress again. It needs another shot at a good time. It's a wonder that he turned up. I'm very glad I'm here. It would be lovely if you were too.

Much love,
Mother

Dearest Amanda,

It's a grizzly cold day outside. The window panes are covered with frost and the snow lies so deep in the driveway that you can't see where the ground dips. It's a nonwork day because of the drifts on the highway and I feel a little at loose ends. Not like a day off from school at all. I don't have a sled anymore and there's no one to play with.

Sometimes on days like this, when the world comes to a blinding halt, I ache for the warmth of the friends and the husband I've lost. Behind me as I write, the room is empty. The whole damn house is empty. It's so quiet and late and I'm so afraid I'm going to be alone, like this, forever.

Rosebud, rosebud. It's hard to remember in the dark that there's a tomorrow.

Stay warm, wrap up, blow your nose, drink some hot chocolate, and hug yourself for me.

I love you.

Mom

Dearest Amanda,

Pardon me while I moan. I've had it. I am up to my ears in disaster. Can you imagine a demand from Gerald that we decipher the slipping market share problem in a matter of five days; a litter of kittens deposited by McMuffin (in my closet as usual, but this time on a De La Renta evening gown that had slipped off its hanger); and a dinner party at which I served take-out Chinese (the caterer came down with some romantic virus that incapacitated him and his staff), all in one week!

After the meeting with Gerald, Jeff Davies and I were sitting in Jeff's office, figuring out how to explore the mysteries of organizational life, when the phone rang. It was his wife, in distress. The furnace was making funny noises. As Jeff asked her to describe the noises, he started packing up his briefcase. It was three-thirty, not too early to leave with a full load of work to do, but he shot a glance at me to see if I'd notice just how full he was cramming his case. I smiled.

"Tell her to turn it off," I said.

"Oh, yeah," Jeff said into the phone, "turn it off.

The switch is at the head of the cellar stairs. The red one. I'll be right home."

Jeff and I made an appointment for the next morning, first thing, he assured me. He fled the office, leaving me to walk back to mine, a sudden victim of disquiet.

The real mystery of organizational life is how it survives at all. Here I am with deadlines, kittens and infectious caterers to worry about and Jeff has a fussy furnace and a wife who doesn't know where the switch is, and yet we are both expected and both expect ourselves to be 100 percent committed to the fortunes of Fairmont, Inc. As I walked back to my office, I tried to figure out what it is that makes an organization like Fairmont go, with its masses of employees all plagued by real and imagined fiery furnaces. In Fairmont's case we can't trace back our answer to Gerald. Efficient as he is, the poor man's so wooden and self-contained he couldn't motivate a bee to buzz around a honey pot. And I suspect that in many organizations, protestations and good incentive programs notwithstanding, what really makes people like Jeff Davies take home piles of paper for the evening (even without my noticing eye) is their own commitment to doing a job well.

In your last letter you mentioned that you are in a quandary over applicants to a position as trainee in your department. From what you say, you're lucky because you have some in-house applicants to choose from, so have a sense of the kinds of people they are. Believe me, choosing the right person is the hardest and most important job you'll perform as manager. Many companies pay lip service to this dictum, but in the flurry of no-show caterers, kittens, unreasonable bosses and exploding furnaces, many of us choose people the way we do a hamburger when we're in a hurry.

Given a range of applicants, what do you look for? As I've said before and as I firmly believe despite the conventional wisdom, it's the ineffables that count most in the long run.

One of the toughest decisions I had to make as a young manager was choosing between two candidates for promotion. Much like the situation you're in, but in my case only two people applied for the job and both were equally qualified. Both were competent and efficient, both extremely bright and pleasant to have around. On the face of it, they were clones. So I chose one over the other based on the feelings I had about the two men. One of them, Harry Finlay, had an office like a laboratory. It was so clean and antiseptic looking that I wouldn't have minded undergoing surgery in it. His desktop was bare and nowhere in the room did you see signs of his occupancy. Joe Epstein's office, on the other hand, was filled with objects he'd brought from home. He had lined one shelf of his bookcase with shells that he collected in Florida, had hung prints on the walls, and had put a nice small Oriental rug on the floor. I felt comfortable when I walked into Joe's office and a little intimidated by Harry's spartan cell.

Joe Epstein had made a commitment to the office as a place he wanted to be, as if he'd be there for a spell. Harry Finlay treated his office as a way station that it wasn't important to make his. Obviously the point of view I took reflects my own biases, and hooray to that, but we do make a statement about our expectations and feelings of belonging to a place (as well as to people) by what we bring to it. Joe's office made the office more homey for me.

You can't, of course, hire someone on the merits of office decor. But people give you all sorts of clues about their involvement. Most of them boil down to whether they let you know them. In the case of Joe, it turned out that my hunch was correct. Joe Epstein is still with the company and Harry Finlay, I found out later, moved from job to job year after year. True, had he got the promotion he might have stayed with us longer, but I didn't make the wrong choice.

Joe won out because I thought he was committed. It also happened that I liked him. But that wasn't necessary. It took me a long time to realize that although it's the best of all possible worlds to like the people you work with, a good subordinate doesn't have to be someone you'd take home to dinner and discuss your intimate fantasies with.

It's not important to like people, but it is important that the people you hire get along. When it comes to appraising their performance, you'll make your judgments according to your comfort level as well as their competence. Most people are reasonably competent, but what makes organizations work like clocks is that people tick. When I worked at Howard, one peer of mine was perfectly competent but he made stupid jokes, laughed inappropriately and talked too much. Such simple social incompetencies sunk him.

It's an issue of trust, and trust is knowledge. Trust is not expecting people to do what you want; it's knowing what they will do. When you are reasonably certain how a person will behave in certain situations, you can be comfortable with that person; you don't have to watch out for the off-color joke told badly. Organizations can tolerate mavericks and need them. But a goofball on a lucky streak doesn't always turn out to be a brilliant individualistic genius. When the behavior is inappropriate or alienating over any period, it's a sure sign of incompleteness in the person and not of a genius at work, whether the person is brilliant or not.

Because you can't completely monitor the people who work for you, and they won't perform for you if you overcontrol them, you have to trust them. So in hiring, look for the people who will let you know them. These people don't run away in conversations, changing the subject or trying to control it; they'll stick with you and become involved. Feeling confident in their right to an opinion, they enjoy the exchange of ideas. They don't shy away from telling you about themselves; they regard feelings as important information (they are!) and don't rationalize them away. They are secure enough to offer you a peek into what they care about. They have the capacity to be attached.

Jeff Davies is a perfect example. To some people it would be problematic that Jeff would leave a meeting with me, nominally his superior, when we're sitting down to discuss an important business issue. And I could tell he felt uneasy about leaving, otherwise he wouldn't have been so blatant about taking so much work home. But because Jeff is involved with his family, he can be involved with work as well. I know Jeff will come in tomorrow morning with a lot of good ideas. He will be thinking about Gerald's problem while he's waiting for the furnace man to come.

An organization is like a family, with sacred goals and values. To join up, people first have to be able to see themselves as belonging to something bigger than themselves. They can't be afraid of mucking in with the masses at work. Overheating furnaces at home can be a sign of generosity and flexibility.

One more thing. No matter how good the employees you hire, they need to know that the organizational family appreciates them. Once you've got the right people, it'll be your job to keep them. Now, how do you think I can get that message across to Gerald? He wants market share to go up and I know that what he wants us to do is fiddle the data. What he needs to do, among many things, is give our people something to believe in. It's awfully hard to want to belong when the family's a bunch of numbers.

Let me know how you fare with your applicants. Give whomever you hire something to work for and he or she will take care of the rest.

Much love,
Mother

May 12

Dearest Amanda,

I loved hearing about your visit with Ginny. Did you really wear a wig? That's fabulous. And she with glasses and a big nose . . . What a pair! What a sight! Give her my best next time you talk.

Remember when you were home last month and we were talking about how your boss got snippy when he asked for your opinion on an investment proposal and you said you weren't sure? He said that he paid you to be sure, or something to that effect. I didn't think much about it at the time, but it occurs to me now that being sure of everything isn't what it's cracked up to be.

A number of years ago, I attended a meeting of one of our divisions where a group of people were discussing a new product idea. I was on a visit so I wasn't going to participate, just observe. The guy running the meeting, Larry Zinn, didn't seem to be running things at all. He spoke rarely while the others bounced ideas back and forth, some ludicrous, some irreverent, some barely ideas at all. The meeting was often interrupted by people bringing in messages to the participants or just dropping by to listen and chime in. Larry Zinn would nod when people spoke, ask a question now and then, but offer nothing himself. After about two hours of this, I was burning to put all the ideas in order and come up with a brilliant overview that would surprise them all and end this seemingly aimless babble. I wanted to astound them with the answer to all their searchings. But because I was only an observer I held back.

At one point someone turned to Zinn and asked, "Do we have an idea?" Larry leaned back in his chair and said, "Maybe." After that I was sure the meeting would end and people would leave feeling disgruntled and unsatisfied, but it didn't seem to. Some people left but others came in, and the talk went on back and forth, some of it having nothing to do with the product idea. They discussed market reports on other items, gossip that one of them had heard about someone in the industry, and the daily special at a favorite restaurant down the street. Finally, Zinn turned to me and asked if I had anything I wanted to add. I had developed an encapsulating statement that I thought would sum up the discussion and point the way, but as I opened my mouth to speak, I realized that my idea would not help the debate along but close it off. I saw I didn't know enough. I said so, feeling it was a bad thing. Expecting scorn, I got a smile.

We broke for lunch, during which the talk continued and I began to throw some hunches into the pot. By the end of the day there was a product idea that everyone agreed to, not by vote but by having arrived at it by this process of not knowing. And they all owned the idea, understood its innards, and assented to it in a way they never would have if it had been offered to them. Larry Zinn simply allowed the idea to be born and by his accepting it gave it legitimacy. Needing to be seen as having the right answer, I would have killed the idea long before it had a shape and consistency of its own. The end of the story is that the product we arrived at never did get off the ground—it faced insuperable manufacturing costs—but it had a short and happy life while it lived, and who knows, it may revive.

With certain business issues—accounting and production control, for instance—systematic rational knowledge is relevant. But when the field shifts and the end is undefined, you have to reshape and refine your idea in a vacuum. In these situations, art not science is what works. When we don't know and don't overplan, the unexpected can occur. The "way" is muddling; taking it means tolerating ambiguity and uncertainty. And, oh, how crucial a strong sense of self is to bear the tension of the unresolved.

So now I should tend to my garden. Oodles of twigs, leaves and last year's dried brown stalks cry for attention. And if I snipped and bunched them, by the end of the day I'd be able to halve my weeding list. Well, bother to that. Today I have another, more important list, which includes walking around the reservoir and seeing if I can spot the deer that live in the woods. Then if I'm lucky the wild iris will be in bloom and I can gaze at them awhile. If they're not, I'll see something else. That's why I like my yard; like not knowing, it has the potential for surprise.

Much love,
Mother

June 22

Dearest Amanda,

Oh, I know just what you mean. It's wonderful to have a man whom you can really talk to and who is interested in what you have to say. At his best, your father was like that. At times we would talk for hours in the morning about anything, a quiet sort of intimacy building between us. We'd lie in bed together holding hands, just chatting away in the dark until we both fell asleep. If you have that with Tom, then you've got something pretty special that makes the hard times worth it. I only hope he knows just how special it is as well.

When your father and I hit the skids, he was somehow able to deny that we'd had those quiet times together. I think that hurt more than almost anything I'd ever experienced. In wiping from his memory all the good times, he denied the best of me. At a distance, I can see now how difficult I must have been for him. I was not happy doing nothing at home after you'd gone to school and I didn't want to have another baby just to fill that gap. The more I itched to do something, the more your father felt I was saying that life with him wasn't enough. It all unraveled so quickly, and he so thoroughly paved over the garden we'd planted.

One of the hardest things for young unmarried or unattached women at work must be the lack of someone to ramble on with in the dead of night, the time when you recharge your emotional batteries and tuck away that special sense of belonging that you can get nowhere else. You know, that might explain some of what you've described going on at Crandall, women colleagues treating business information as just so much fodder for the intimacy cow. Women need attachments in ways men don't, or can't acknowledge. At least most of us have learned to associate acceptance with sharing our feelings, and the line between talking about feelings and passing information is very thin.

I can imagine the scene. You sitting at lunch with a female colleague, creating between you a warm atmosphere bred of the revealing of confidences, and all of a sudden she says, "And just between you and me, Emmy Lou is going to get the Simpatico project. Bill and Brad were discussing it just the other day at lunch. She doesn't deserve it. You do." Because of the process you've just engaged in, the sharing of a secret, you smile, but part of you simmers. You wanted the Simpatico deal, and now you're in possession of partial information that could be misleading. If you're like me, you'll start seeing all sorts of meaning in the conversation between Bill and Brad, and why were they saying this in front of this gossip before you knew you'd been beaten out for the job?

All hypothetical, of course, but I've seen this happen so often between women. The motivation is closeness, but the result can be misuse of communication networks. I've even done it myself, on the grubby days when not being alone is worth any price.

Don't indulge in this game. Ask yourself what you really want out of the conversation. A few points on the intimacy scale? If so, clamp your hand over your mouth as fast as you can; you're sucking at the wrong breast. There's nothing wrong in talking about your personal lives with others whom you trust. One of the great gifts women bring to the male world of business is a willingness to engage in relationships that have more than business as the bottom line. But don't trade gossip for closeness; people will stop talking to you and legitimate informal channels of communication will dry up for you.

Isn't it odd? I found that when my life with your father was going well and I didn't have much bitching and moaning to indulge in, many of my friends had little to say to me, and I to them. I wondered about that and it frightened me a bit. So much of the conversation between women is built up on what to do about a man, or how to please one, that when this is not an issue there seems little to talk about. It's almost as if we deny each other's worth as women and as friends if we try to talk about something else.

After your father left and I started at Fairmont, I desperately needed friends to talk to about the difficulties I was having here, but they couldn't understand. I suppose it's different now that so many women are working. Thank God for the new experiences to talk about. Maybe through all this, women will become able to base friendship more on shared interests—and men will learn to express how they feel. Women can't use the business world as an emotional or a sexual playground and succeed; it will mark them forever as "just women" when what they want is to be taken seriously for the good things they have to offer. For every woman who gossips or screws her way up the ladder, another will get screwed.

And on that delicate and totally bald appraisal of the state of the art, I leave you. Oh—your Aunt Sally is going to be in New York at the end of the month and would love to see you. She asked me for your number, so will probably call. She knew your father pretty well in the early days and so may be able to give you some perspective on him that I can't. I had to seal up that wound so long ago, I'm still not sure I have it right. She's also seen him, I think, so you might learn more about what he's up to.

Isn't this funny—after this long letter about women and their talk about men, here I am doing it. It's never wrong to be interested in men, thank heaven; we just need to develop other things to talk about as well. Like clothes? Joke, joke! How's your backhand??

Much love,
Mother

Dearest Amanda,

What a question! You really make me stop and think. How did I get to the top? First of all, the notion that there is a top unsettles me some. I suppose there is, in an objective sense, if you look at an organization as a hierarchy and a series of boxes and lines, but no organization that I know of operates that way. Oh, I guess some managers see their companies in these terms, and boxes and lines are a help when sorting out messes, but when everything goes the way it should, they mean very little. Also, a top implies a bottom, and these are loaded words; top usually means better than bottom. And thinking that way really doesn't get one very far. I prefer to think of an organization as a circle rather than a triangle (how very female of me), with the people in the outer ring having more responsibility because they encompass more, but not being more important.

Anyway, that's my personal prejudice, but it may be a clue to how to answer your question. First of all, being in the outer ring requires that you have a general management perspective. You consider the needs and requirements not only of one of the circles but of all of them. You don't see marketing as more important than manufacturing, or your customers as more important than your employees. They are all necessary to the success of an organization, and managing at outer levels requires that a person resolve issues in the best interests of all the different groups. Sounds straightforward, but I'm convinced it takes a breadth of vision to do this juggling act day after day, making more correct balances than lopsided ones. And here, I think (God, this is going to sound immodest as hell and I blush a little as I write), is where who you are counts for more than what you know (although that is important too). Let me expand a little on that one. (It's sort of fun, working this out this way. I've never really thought of it before, so be prepared for stumbles and false starts.)

Having an overview means seeing the big picture. And having the capacity to see the big picture means that your individual interests sometimes have to take a back seat. To do this you must have your personal needs and quirks in perspective, having acquired sufficient personal integrity or maturity to perceive events that occur as affecting the whole, not just yourself. For instance, in your letter you wonder whether I had difficulty chumming up with male superiors, whether being a woman made it hard for me to be accepted. Well, of course, it did at first, but I think that once my male superiors saw that I was not out for myself but had the greater good in mind, most of them treated me normally.

This is hard to explain. I didn't brush up on the front line of the Green Bay Packers, nor did I force people

52

to talk in terms of nurturance and support. I never was a supermotivated achiever. I took jobs because they were offered to me and did well at them because while I was there it seemed reasonable to do as well as I could (it was going to take nearly the same amount of time to do something badly as to do it well). No, what got me accepted, I think, was that I wasn't out for myself and that I didn't see myself as not being equal to the men above me. It has simply rarely occurred to me that if I went somewhere I couldn't talk and make sense with most people I met.

When I went for my job interview at Fairmont, after the divorce, when things were pretty scrappy, not much money in the bank, and you at home to support, I needed the job badly. And my state of mind was not the best. I wasn't sure I wanted to work for a large manufacturing company that made things as exciting as screwdrivers and levels. But I knew I needed a job and that I wouldn't get it if I presented myself as a hungry, nervous rabbit. I had about three hundred dollars in the bank. Most of it should have gone for rent and food, but I spent it all on a new dress, shoes, handbag, underwear and (can you believe this?) gloves. I went dressed to the nines, knowing that how I felt about myself would determine how the interview went. It did.

The chief of the department met with me, but we didn't have a formal interview, we simply talked. He asked if I thought I'd be able to handle top executives that I'd meet in the course of my work, and I remember being surprised by the question. Of all the things that I would have to do to perform a job, it never occurred to me that this would be difficult. I took it for granted. It's an ease,

53

Amanda, an ease with people of all sorts that gets you to the top. It's knowing that it's okay for you to be where you are, so that you don't have to step on the heads of people below you to prove it.

Of course, functional expertise in an area, such as you're developing in investments and planning, will take you quite a way. But what makes you part of the outer circle is your sense of yourself as belonging there. If you belong, you don't have to elbow your way in; you walk through the door. And it's just a matter of time before others see this quality in you. The quality is self-assurance based on self-knowledge.

True, I'm glossing over a lot of the little insecurities that washed over me on the way up. At times I was afraid to try new things and often felt, even when I'd done a wonderful job, that I'd never be able to repeat the success and would have to start from zero.

But as successes became more frequent, I began to see the qualms for just what they were, fruits borne of competing in a male world. And many of the qualms were of my own making, not theirs (although there were unaccountable unhelpful dolts who would reinforce them along the way).

It's still easier for me to receive a woman's serve in tennis than a man's. Not because it's softer, but because I have no ambivalance about really hitting out at it. But in the main, if you see yourself as belonging in the game, you can return more serves than you fluff even when the server is a man, even a very handsome one. (That adds an interesting wrinkle that I'll try to iron out in another letter.)

Right now I've got a meeting to go to and Peggy's drumming her fingers on the corner of my desk. She says to say hi. Let me know what you think of these thoughts of mine; many of them are new to me. Thanks for asking.

Much love,
Mother

August 2

Dearest Amanda,

Dammit. You're not going to let me off so easily. Yes, of course working my way up was hard, but it's a different kind of hard than working twelve hours a day is, which is what I think you meant. I never started out my career with a career in mind, the way you are. I never took all the years at Howard seriously. I always felt, the way many women in those days did, that eventually I'd get married, have children, and boom, it would be over. Working was something you did between the major attachments of your life. Eventually it dawned on me that I'd work forever because I wanted to and it was gratifying.

But I don't think I ever worked for the signs of success in the outside world: Positions, trappings of power, titles, money, all bespeak achievement. There's only one way to really succeed and that's inside. It's the inside world that counts, knowing that you are in there with your heart and soul, not just half of you making a passing toss of your hat into the ring. I know when I hold back. In sex it's pretty obvious—you don't have an orgasm (that assumes a reasonably competent partner). On the tennis court, your feet just don't move fast enough and your mind wanders, so that you're a millisecond too slow going after the ball. At work, you arrive at nine and go through the motions, but what do you initiate?

Reasons abound to explain why we hold back from performing as well as we could. A lot of the doubt about what I could achieve may well have been because I was working with men who seemed to make a big deal about achievement and made it difficult for others, especially women. The environment we work in has a hell of a lot to do with how we perceive ourselves.

I can remember my first week here. Because I'd been hired by the chief, who liked the cut of my three-hundred-dollar jib, I was immediately suspect as his mouthpiece, his favorite. No one asked me to lunch. At the end of the first week, I went into the office of one of these close-mouthed mammoths and asked if anyone ever spoke to anyone else. He looked at me across his desk of neatly stacked papers and said, in words that became etched in my brain, "Business is a lonely business." In the very early days here, whenever I asked a simple question because I did not know the answer, the eyes of my peers would start their scheduled flight around the room, inevitably landing on the ceiling. Then there'd be a collective sigh.

How did I like it? Not at all. I almost quit Fairmont after the first month, it was so bad. It was Peggy who saved my life. She was a secretary for one of the guys downstairs.

She came to my office one day and told me that all the men were suspicious of me and that they'd never make a move in my direction, that if I was going to succeed here I'd have to take the first step. I was furious at first. Here I was the victim of obvious stereotypical discrimination, supposedly someone the bloody place had hired to be of help, and I was being totally iced.

I stewed for a few days, weighing the benefits of quitting vs. screaming at my boss vs. crying. I felt like a rape victim being asked to console her raper for his guilt. But this is what you have to do if you're going to succeed in a situation like this, because the bloody oafs simply don't know any better. So I began a subtle courtship of each and every man on the hall. Not a sexual courtship—I was very conscious of playing down the sexual completely—but a social one. I avoided as much as possible in the first months asking business questions, figuring I'd do better to try to piece out the right way to do things myself. I'd check old reports for guidelines on writing things up, listen carefully to how others presented things, and read more damn material on machinery than I'd known existed. No, my courtship was for friends or anyway people to eat with, to feel at least partially at home with.

It happened very slowly. I'd drop by someone's office, never enter it, lean against the doorjamb and ask a nonbusiness question. I asked more damn stupid questions, but it put them at their ease about me. I wasn't showing myself to be a baby about work and I wasn't pushing my sex at them. Slowly, like the dawning of the sun after the ice age, they'd begin to respond with a question of their own as they leaned against my doorjamb. One or two made the brave step across my threshold. Eventually three of them asked me to lunch. It took three!

And I think it took six months, maybe a year, before I could ask a business question straight without fearing that the man I asked it of would sigh and raise his eyes to the ceiling. It's so pointless, this hazing, but there's no way women on their own aren't going to go through it. This is why I keep harping on the inner strength bit, on the feeling deep in your bones that you belong. Because if you don't have it, the worst of them can scare you out. I stayed because I would not be pushed out by my own fury at *their* fear.

After that the sea was calmer. I felt in, part of the gang, when doing the work well became the main concern of my day. Being accepted as a person became the same thing as being accepted for my work. When I think back on it, I was the holdout. It took me a long time to decide finally to marry this bunch of goons after the "beautiful" courtship I'd had. And I fear that this is a problem many women still experience. We work so bloody hard to be accepted as people that we're bound to be furious underneath. And I am convinced that fury is what makes us still feel outsiders long after the "dear" men we work with have begun to see us as simply people. They know not what they did. Numbers of senior women have admitted the same thing to me, and it's a sad commentary. It's not until they've reached a certain point in an organization that they can afford to realize how angry and bitter they've been. And this is too bad, because it means that for a long time they weren't giving their all, they were holding back something along the line. I don't know what more I could have done to compensate for my own anger. This is why I am so vigilant about sabotage and hang back; that way lies a deep dreary funk. Activity is its own reward.

And my reward today is a long lunch with Jeff Davies and Chip Rosen. We're taking the afternoon off to go to a baseball game. I'm going to get sick on hot dogs. Can't resist them.

Much love,
Mother

P.S. What happened with Tom? It sounded like such a lovely time you were having together, where you were beginning to relax. Why don't you call him and find out? If he's got a bad case of the male disease, running from mother in the kitchen, he may well see the phone call as pushy and evidence that you're his mother's clone, but you need that piece of information, don't you think? Oh, God, it's so hard, but try not to fit his needs so much. It's what you need that's important. These things get no easier as you get older, believe me. Well, that's not altogether true; as we age, we get less afraid of these panics and see them as simply panics. But I find myself, on the edge of a dinner date with Bill Rawlings, suddenly excited and afraid too. And then I think that there's nothing to fear but facing the feast alone, and I've done that—oh, how I've done that.

Dearest Amanda,

I can understand your being put out by Tom's wanting to go camping for a week, but try seeing it in his terms. He may very likely need time away to be able to be close. The looser the tie for a man, sometimes the stronger it is.

What's it like to be a man? Good God, I don't know. Sometimes I think that the similarities between men and women far outweigh the differences and other times I think we are so different it's amazing that we walk on the same planet during the same geological era. We all look for love and affection and approval, need sleep, need food, and need warmth in the winter and cool breezes in the summer. But we've been socialized to believe in a difference: Girls are women from the day they are born, while boys are not men. Obviously, the thinking goes, little girls aren't women in the sense of being able to bear children, but they turn into women in their sleep. One day they wake up and they've got blood in their pants and it's done. We don't have to do anything but sit around and wait for it to happen, and happen it does. Passivity personified.

But for a boy to become a man, he has to do something. He has to have an impact on the outside world. Look at the way we talk about men and women. We talk about telling the men from the boys. We never speak of telling the girls from the women; it's a boring exercise. But, you may say, little boys come with the same physical equipment that men have, and overnight their voices drop and they grow hair on their chests without doing anything, so why do they need to have an impact?

Boys have to distinguish themselves from their mothers and forge an identity with their fathers. Girls have to become separate from their mothers to grow, but they don't need to acquire a new sexual identity to do it. Boys do. And what an enormous job that must be. What they're shooting for—Dad—seems so far away. I wouldn't know how to go about it. Imagine trying to become something quite different from what you are. It would be as if at a certain age, ten, I'd said to you, okay, Amanda, go out and grow hair on your chest. How would you begin to go about it? In many ways, what women today are going through is similar. They're trying new things with very little idea of what to do. But we don't—at least I didn't—have to match a superwoman. And for many women today, there's still nothing to prove; it's a given. Just think what it would be like if you had to prove it beyond what you already have at your disposal. How terrifying. And what if you couldn't do it, what if you had no way to make anyone believe you were really a woman? It's still unthinkable, isn't it? For us the question doesn't arise in the same way.

So let's imagine trying to develop a new sex. Well, you look around and see the things that mothers do, and,

God, you don't want to do them. You don't want to be passive, hug too much, be weak, short—(I ask you, what's the big deal about short men? The only possible thing wrong is that women are "short" and men are "tall," so it must be something you don't want to be.) Given that mandate, what would you do? I'd go out and hit things. That's one way not to be passive. I'd throw things, I'd yell a lot and make a lot of noise. I'd move fast, faster than Mom. So I'd probably hit the road a lot, first on a bike, then in a car, and I'd drive it fast. I'd play a lot of tough games so that I was physically stronger and I'd make sure that I was as strong as the others of this new sex, so I'd probably challenge them to fights. Because, brother, I'm not going to be a weak son-of-a-bitch like a woman.

Now, say I accomplish all these things. (Meanwhile, notice how my language has become a little hostile. The woman has become the enemy for a while here. I'm afraid of her because she's a powerful pull in the wrong direction, though because I'm not supposed to be afraid of anything, I don't show it overtly. Instead I treat her offhandedly and put a distance between us. I've got other things on my mind.) Okay. I've got a separate sex, but then there's that big guy, Dad, way out ahead of me. He's still bigger and stronger than I am. More work to do.

I am full of admiration. It's quite simply a breathtaking thing that men do. And all of them try to do it and some of them fail. That's not very surprising.

It sure makes sense to me that the men at Crandall, like the men at other corporations, would be reluctant to let women into their strongholds. Remember when you tried to invade Danny Simmons' fort, and he and Billy

Shaw got so mad? Didn't they move the fort a couple of times until you and Sylvia couldn't find it? Is it really surprising that some of the men at Crandall are shifty when talking to you, keep bits of information away, and try to downplay your abilities? And in some ways I think you're probably having it tougher than I did. I was an aberration. The oddball, the exception that proved the rule. You know that when I started working I didn't worry about wearing three-piece suits and carrying attaché cases like my male peers, or keeping my hair ruly or not appearing feminine. It was obvious what I was, and because I was the oddball and accepted, the whole package got through. I didn't wear dresses slit to my navel, but I didn't worry about looking "businesslike."

But now I understand all the dress-for-success books. You women have to creep up on the fort in disguise, or else they'll move it on you. Christ, an army of you is coming over the hill, all equipped with attaché cases containing scissors and knives and all sorts of emasculating equipment. Hell, I'd move the fort too! There is safety in numbers for the women, but believe me, no safety for the men—not now, not yet.

In the meantime, just because they have the fort, try not to see men as the enemy. Be assertive and straightforward but not aggressive. It can fall flat. I was at a lunch once, all men and me, and one of the men told a dirty joke. So I replied in kind. It was a good joke, but drew no laughs.

Oops. I'm late for a meeting. I'll continue this later.

Much love,
Mother

P.S. I'm dying to hear about the new job with Peter Shell. I had a feeling we hadn't heard the last of that probing a year ago. Hooray for you. When did Crandall get into the acquisition business? Isn't that a new direction?

Dearest Amanda,

Oh, ick. What a jerk! He honestly locked the door, started plumping up the cushions on the couch, and asked you to join him "in pleasure"? That's a new one! It must have been a little frightening and at the same time infuriating. It sounds as if you handled it well, but what is this nonsense about you having been partly to blame? Good Lord, you go to see someone in his office and he starts making moves on you and you're at fault? I can understand your feeling that way because you might have to deal again with this person who's got more power in the organization than you do. But you're not powerless in this world and you can affect how he'll treat you.

When I started out at Fairmont, I worked for a man (who shall remain nameless to protect the guilty, because he's still here and I don't see any reason to drag his poor ego through the mud, where it lives most of the time anyway) who in most respects was easy to get along with. I liked him and learned from him quite a lot about how things work around here. I saw him as a friend, so when we went to Washington on business and stayed at a hotel and had dinner together and a few drinks afterward, perfectly amicably and businesslike, and he asked me to his room to go over some papers before the meeting the next morning, I went along qualmless.

I know you're not going to believe this, I hardly do myself, but it's true. I was sitting in a chair, reading, when he sat down on the edge of the bed and made a little speech. He was glad I was there and hoped that I'd go along with an experiment he had in mind. He proposed that we take off our clothes and then sit in the two chairs on either side of the small table by the windows and continue doing our work. Our being naked would, of course, create some anxiety and tension for the two of us, but—and here was the experiment—we would try to overlook our nakedness and overcome the anxiety and work despite our discomfort and growing passion. In this way we would learn control and how to handle our nervousness. This would be good training for all business situations. If we could do this, we'd be able to sit through anything without feeling panic.

"That's a good idea," I said, "but I don't think it will work."

"Why not?" he said.

"Because," I said, "I think it would add a dimension to our relationship that we should not add."

"Not if it works. If it works we'll be able to rise above everything."

"Yes," I said, "that's true, but if it doesn't work, one of us has to weaken first and that one will be in a terrible position of being seen by the other as having less control. And as control is the point, that would really interfere with how we will be able to work together in the future."

Wasn't that a brilliant response? Even as I think of it, I'm struck by my own creativity under pressure. At the time, I saw three needs. One was to get out of there, second was to keep his dignity intact, and third was to keep my cool. Here is the hard part. Despite the absurdity of it all, there was something in me that was tempted to go along. *Not* because I was overcome with passion and found him desirable (that would have been an interesting problem), but because it would have taken care of my feeling of impotence and the fury it created. Because he was my boss and had power over me, I not only was the victim but also was the one who had in that situation to preserve the relationship.

And this is, I am convinced, why so many women who are victims of sexual harassment report feeling dirty and a bit crazy. If you can't see any reasonable way out of a situation, the solution, as old as slavery, is to adopt the point of view of the aggressor, and go along. If the aggressor is right, how can you be angry at him? The angrier you are and the more impotent, the stronger the need to identify, I imagine, when there's no way out (Patty Hearst would be an extreme example).

The trick then is to preserve a sense of power. Fortunately, sexual harassment is actionable, so if things really get tough, you can take the creep to court. But short of that, for the one-timers, it helps to see the sexual come-on as a power play. Keep your response organizational. Don't answer in personal terms. Use the organization as your ally. Tell him that it would affect how you work together and that would hurt your performance for the company. Put your joint responsibility to the organization first. Unless he's completely nuts, he'll see the reason in your response. In this way you'll rebuff him not because he's a drooling nincompoop but because he does have power. And face it, these guys are doing what they're doing because they're threatened by you (as well as attracted), and the best thing is to make them feel less threatened by handing them gobs of glorious power all sugared up with concern for the company and all that crap. It works.

The one thing you can't do is remain silent. Some men will see silence as passivity and interpret it as acceptance. When one of these people tries again, which he will, and you really get pushed into a corner and have to fight back, he won't understand it. And in a way, why should he? Most guys aren't aware of what they're doing when they indulge in this sort of sexualized power play. So make sure you are understood.

As for the one-liners, the "Gee, I wouldn't mind climbing these stairs if I had your legs to do it with," you'll hear them until your legs drop off. Treat it as a bad joke, and don't laugh. Of course, if the guy is an equal, let him have it, gently between the eyes.

Enough of this. How are you otherwise? I don't mean to pry (yes, I do) but you haven't mentioned Tom or any other man for a long time. What gives?

> Much love,
> *Mother*

Dearest Amanda,

I have some bad news. I got up this morning and went down to the kitchen to make some coffee before taking a shower, and Sheba was lying in the middle of the floor, inert and solid looking. I thought for a moment that she had just decided that the kitchen rug was the best place to take an early morning nap and that she'd bounce up in a moment and ask to be let out. I even got as far as measuring the coffee into the pot before I could adjust my sight to see what I really didn't want to see. She wasn't moving. She hadn't greeted me with her customary thump of tail; she wasn't there at all. I stood staring at her glossy coat laid out like a silky offering and willed her to move, but she didn't. I bent over her and put my ear to her chest, but there was nothing. She was already quite stiff.

Mr. Harrison helped me get her into the car and I got her over to Dr. Kent's. There was nothing to do for her, of course; she had died in the night, peacefully, he guessed, of heart failure. I hadn't realized in all these years that Sheba was getting on and would die someday, just like that, no barking to announce her departure, no last wag of the tail or intense look from those brown eyes. She hadn't even made it up the stairs to my room to say goodbye. Because these thoughts are the ultimate in anthropomorphic and don't suit, I am trying to look at death in her terms. She didn't know she was going anywhere at all. All she did was lie down; it was that simple.

I left her at Dr. Kent's and came home. When I came in the back door, McMuffin was sipping water from Sheba's bowl. Then, fearing detection from Sheba, she took a swipe at the wet food in the dish and carried it off in a crablike run to her own lair. I suppose for a while McMuffin will think that Sheba is merely in another room or out in the yard playing a perpetual hide-and-seek. And then she will forget. I'm feeling like the elephant around here this morning. I'll find it hard. And part of me keeps saying, If only I hadn't seen, it wouldn't have happened and I wouldn't be feeling this ache, not for her but for me. Is that why sometimes it's so hard to see, because we are afraid we can't stand the pain and all the past losses the next moment will bring?

I didn't want to tell you this because I know you're feeling miserable about Tom. From the sound of it, he just isn't able to make you the priority in his life that you would like, and that's so disappointing. Although it's hard, we need to grieve. For me the difficulty is that I associate grieving with my having done something wrong. Should I have noticed that something was amiss with Sheba when she didn't come up the stairs last night? I don't think so really, any more than you should feel inadequate because Tom withdrew. If I can stand my own imperfection, it's easier to mourn, and grieving is the only way to stay true to both the person lost and yourself. I'm so very sorry about Tom. Listen to me going back and forth trying to comfort us both when the only comfort for me right now comes in admitting how terribly sad I am. You too?

Take care of that cold. You sounded absolutely awful on the phone, or were you being brave and pretending you weren't crying? I'm glad I'm writing this and not talking; I don't think I'd get a word out. What a letter. I'll write more later, tomorrow maybe, when I can see.

Much love,
Mother

March 24

Dear One,

How was *Tristan and Isolde?* I find the music almost unbearably beautiful; it hurts to hear it. Did you wear the amethysts? They were your grandmother's and she gave them to me the night your father and I went off in full regalia to hear *Tristan.* What a time we had! We both got drunk on champagne and left after the second act to go home and conceive you. So the amethysts have been yours all along. I've only been safeguarding them. They have magic. Happy night that was. Happy birthday again.

Love love love,
Mom

Dearest Amanda,

I'm staying in a cottage overlooking a strand of beach, empty except for a few stray bullocks, which are little bulls, if ever a bull can be little, and next to sloping green fields where sheep leap at the slightest sound. I think there was a picture of this place in one of your fairy tale books. Remember the brownie doll you had for years until the moths destroyed its face? Well, this is where all brownies come from. They live in the hills behind the cottage. Seriously.

I got the sweater you wanted, except you're not going to want it. It's a bilious green and rank still with sheep oil. It's so greasy that when I wore it yesterday in the rain—just to test it out, mind, not a serious wearing—I smelled myself coming down the road and had to go the other way. How Irish of me, and how easily learned this inside-out way of approaching things. If you insist on keeping the sweater, I suppose you can. Just in case, I got two.

I bought them at the original cottage of cottage

industries. I had to walk about three miles off the road to find the place where I'd been assured the best sweaters were made. When I got there it was late afternoon and two old women were sitting outside by the front door, knitting. They barely made notice of me. I stood watching them knit, not knowing what to say, and they clearly didn't want to start any conversation with me. I wondered at how they manage to sell anything; their marketing techniques are awful. I was about to say something when one of them got up and went inside and returned with an armful of sweaters. After a minute I knew why the nonexistent sell works. The sweaters are beautifully made. Each sweater is an individual statement by the woman who made it.

I could have bought them all. But I honestly felt it would have been greedy; there aren't many little old women like those two left.

As I walked back, ever on the lookout for peaked hats in the gorse bushes, I wondered what makes these women go on knitting? Sure, they need the money, and I suppose the pounds I left there (the transaction is not a "sale") will take them a ways, but inflation is rampant and it's not going to buy them diamonds and pearls to cast before their swine. (Did I mention the pigs?) Sure and it isn't the lovely working conditions, although I'm not certain about that one. Sitting outside in the late afternoon sun by a whitewashed wall under the eaves of a thatched roof could be idyllic. But the inside of the cottage is dark and damp, and winter there must be awful. So let's scratch working conditions as an incentive. Now, they don't have a bully of a supervisor standing over them, unless the customer assumes that role—I guess I did for a bit. It leaves

72

me with the inescapable conclusion that they make the sweaters because they're good at it and like knitting.

How do you make people care about what they do? Aha, I caught myself. You don't make them, you can't *make* people care about what they do; concern is something they have to give freely.

When I returned to work, after you'd gone off to school and before I joined Fairmont, I worked in a department store for six months. (Remember when I used to bring you goldfish?) It was a small store and many of the salaried employees did double duty supervising the hourly people. I was put in charge of a group of four women whose job was sorting stubs that clerks had ripped off items when they rang up the purchase on the cash register. It was a double-check procedure, for the inventory lists, and about as boring and useless a dumb job as I could imagine. About once a week I'd force myself to check into the basement sorting room—say "Hi" to the women there, see how things were going, and try to show interest.

One day I walked into the room and one of the workers, a large woman named Rosa, glared at me across the table of boxes she was putting her stubs into. (I ate dinner once at a house where the host had his Doberman pinscher chained in the corner of the dining room. It kept straining against its leash all during the dinner, making silent snapping gestures with its mouth. Rosa looked like that.)

"Why do you bother to come down here?" she said. "We're not snitching anything."

"Of course you're not snitching anything," I answered, my back to the wall. "I come down here because it's part of my job." Sometimes supreme candor elicits the same. There was no point in bluffing with Rosa.

"Well, you sure don't like your job much," she said. "Why don't you quit?"

Rosa sat back in her stiff little chair and laughed. The three other women, who'd kept their heads down during this little encounter with truth, joined Rosa's laughter, except theirs was a more snickering, less full-bellied kind.

"Why don't *you?*" I snapped back, pit terrier to her Doberman.

"I like *my* job," she said, with great emphasis.

Her meaning was unmistakable. It was me she didn't like much. I was assailed by a million instincts at once, fight, flee and cry among them.

"That's nice," I said finally. "You're good at it."

Rosa looked at me, her fat creased face suddenly less frightening. "Thank you," she said. She put her head down and continued sorting stubs into the boxes. "See you later," I said, and left.

You know, I've managed people for twenty years and I still forget that I don't have to want to do what they do to like them or respect them for doing it. I slip into the elitist guilt-fed trap of thinking that I'd have to like performing a job in order to think it's worthwhile. And, of course, the people actually doing the work sense that. Rosa had a real nose for my contempt, bless her.

After that we became buddies of a sort. I'd go down there with my coffee and sticky roll and hang out with Rosa, Helen, Marjorie and Frances, and gossip and chat about kids and the price of butter. We never discussed work; there wasn't much to talk about. When there was, it came up naturally, like the time Helen angrily heaved a whole handful of stubs on the floor. The perforations on the stubs had been done inadequately, so that when the cashier ripped them, the stubs got torn, making it hard for Helen to read the department number. Frances suggested that *they* (you know who *they* is) color-code the stubs. That solved the problem easily. If I'd persisted in confusing my job with theirs, we'd never have found that out.

I left the department store not long after we changed the colors. Rosa was right; I really didn't like my job that much. They're probably long gone as well; some computer is checking the inventories. I don't imagine the computers talk about their kids or teach callow, snobby young managers much about the worth of jobs.

You're sounding like you like *your* job. But it does seem as if you're shooting blind. Can't Shell get your CEO to be more specific in his acquisition objectives? I would think it awfully difficult to study prospects without a clear picture of what kind of fit you're looking for, both technological and marketing. Or does Crandall just want to be a big conglomerate? Seems it would be crucial to know. Can't you push Shell a little?

How are other things? I want to ask about Tom, of course, but don't want to as well. If it's really giving you a tough time, do you think you might want to see someone about it? What a euphemism! I don't know whether we really ever talked much about your daddy's leaving. It was so hard for me and I feel so remiss about that because it may have left you with some ideas about men, and me too. What do you think?

Miss you lots. If you ever get a chance to visit this place, do. You may have to see me again.

Much love,
Mother

May 14

Dearest Amanda,

Hey diddle diddle the cat and the fiddle your mom jumped over the moon. So pleased to hear about your promotion! Don't bother checking out Fairmont; we're ungovernable. Would that be a conflict of interest? What a first! We'd make the front page of the *Wall Street Journal* for sure.

I looked for photographs of your father and came up with the enclosed. I like especially the two of you in the tire. That must be Indian Pond. You were four. God, you look alike. Why should I be surprised? Have I been enough of a parent for you? What a question! What could you answer? Our time as a family together was so short and uncollected, like this letter.

Saw *Ordinary People* the other night. It's gruesome in its reality and splendid in its unblinking depiction of the empty cupboards we feed from. There's no getting around how responsible we mothers are.

Much love,
Mother

Dearest Amanda,

For a change—I know you won't believe it's possible—you're going to find me at a loss for words.

This is difficult because I am so afraid that what I want to say you'll take as a real maternal put-down, and it's not meant to be. I'm as aware as you are how some mothers can't stand their daughters' competing with them, and I suppose if I searched the slimy caverns of my soul I'd find lurking in the dimness a horrid creature that would chortle at your troubles and shrivel at your successes. But as I sit here searching the far corners, looking for the creature's spoor, I find none. But of course, that's no guarantee, is it, and that's what's giving me such a hard time.

I'll have to finish this later. I'm stuck. . . .

Bear with me. I do want you to succeed in everything you try, but more important, I want you to enjoy yourself in the process. And this is not a secret wish that you fail, please believe me. It is instead an avowed hope that you aim for doing things right as well as getting the "right" things done. Does that make sense? It's the old question of means vs. ends. (It must have been a diabolical sort who tried to differentiate them in the first place.)

Now the hard part. Why am I writing you about this? I'm worried about your desire to "succeed" and am afraid you will lose sight of how to go about it. My evidence is pretty flimsy, but there was something in the way you described your acquisition prospects that made it seem as if you see them, as well as anyone who disagrees, as the enemy. Is your point to acquire good companies that will enhance Crandall's position, or to succeed? Oh, God, this is a ticklish business and I feel way out on a limb here because I don't know all the specifics and have only feeling to go by.

Okay, I won't mince words. You described writing a report to Bradley Crane, who I assume is Peter Shell's immediate superior. (What does that make him—director of corporate planning?) In any event, in the report you were supposed to describe a company and your reasons for thinking that it's a good prospect. Fair enough. But it doesn't sound as if it turned out the way you hoped. Instead of accepting the report and congratulating you on how well it was put together, Bradley Crane told you to go back and write it again, this time with an eye to convincing him of the merits of the company rather than beating him over the head, or words to that effect.

Amanda, listen carefully to what he's saying. He may be right and may not be the personification of the ugly

78

male superior that you would believe him to be. I know, I don't know, and Bradley Crane may be simply unbearable, but something is amiss here. Did you write that report in a fighting mood, assuming that you'd have to convince Crane with bludgeons rather than with evidence that the company is a good buy? While you console yourself with a lot of feminist hyperbole about bad bosses keeping women in their place, it may be that he's telling you something about the way you do things, not just what you do.

How do I know? Simply because a similar thing happened to me. I had to write a request for a promotion for Chip Rosen once when my boss Jack Gammino was at Harvard doing the advanced management course. I saw getting Chip the promotion as a big deal (Jack hadn't been able to do it) and set out with sword raised to assault the personnel office. An assault it was, and Chip's raise hung by a thread (he did deserve it, just as your company might well be a terrific purchase) because in the process I had implied that the people in the personnel office were dolts who couldn't recognize a valuable employee the way I could.

I was angry before I put a foot in the personnel department door, and it sounds to me as if you were angry, expecting a fight, in describing your prospect to Crane. What a turnabout! Just because it has been a struggle for women to succeed—and no one in their right mind is going to dispute that—it doesn't mean that the way to get things accomplished is to do battle. The male stereotype may not be the best thing to emulate in all cases. People who succeed (and so far most of them have been men) don't do it by putting up a barrage and storming the offices of the people they need to influence. Images to the contrary, men don't succeed that way, and women, with even a heavier load to carry, definitely don't.

So many women think fighting is the way, rather than seeing that agreement is the means as well as the end and that they need to use the system, imperfect as it is, to achieve that agreement. Bradley Crane is part of the system. Use his expertise and experience; don't run him over.

This is very difficult, because it's so easy to see the obstacles and sometimes people in positions over you will be obdurate and put up hurdles just for the fun of seeing you try to leap them. But women make a mistake when they adapt that way of being as a guide. A few years ago, I was conducting a telephone survey of members of a marketing association. This is not an exaggeration. Every man I called either answered his own phone or called me back in person when I couldn't reach him. Every woman had a secretary answer the phone or place the return call. Of course, that's a fluke: Many men have secretaries place calls for them— sometimes it's the most efficient thing to do. Still, all the women, every damn one of them, acted out the old male stereotype about power and availability. (I don't have to tell you which members of the association will probably get my attention in the future.) It's been my experience working with women that they think this "powerful" behavior will make them seem more like successful men, when in fact it's this behavior, which is really based on perceived lack of power, on a sense that they don't really belong, that keeps them more separate. It doesn't make them seem like successful people, but more like entitled children. As you can see, I'm beating my same old drum again.

How you can tell whether you're doing it right is by how you feel. When I charged into the personnel office, I wasn't having a good time. When you're up for a fight, fun doesn't enter into it. This is why I said I want you to enjoy yourself. It's the best guarantee there is that you're operating with a full sense of your own worth and therefore don't have to play power games with others. It is a challenge to get things accomplished, but exercising your skills should be a pleasure, not something about which you have to grit your teeth and snarl.

Amanda, I'm sorry if this makes you angry, but what I suggest is that you check with Bradley Crane. Ask him what he meant. Give him a chance, and yourself too. Anger is so exhausting, and staying angry won't get the report rewritten in a way that he'll accept.

Chip did get the raise, by the way, after I backed off and dealt with the facts, not the feelings. When Jack got back he was amazed at my "success." But it was really by not "trying to be successful" that I achieved what I wanted.

How did the dinner party go? Did the beef Wellington pastry work out all right? Millie wanted me to remind you that a cup of brown flour is a must to get the right consistency, and of course I forgot. Save both our hides: When you write her next, include a wee bit of the brown in your report. I am so impressed by how well you cook. Millie deserves all the credit for that, not me. Do you remember the time you and I made that cake for your class party and the frosting came out submarine gray? You were so unflapped by it, when I thought you had every right to throw a tantrum. But take it off to your party you did, such a brick you were, and so was the cake, probably.

Much love,
Mother

Dearest Amanda,

Just a quick note to tell you that Peggy's fine. The tests show nothing, though I still worry about her. She seems so tired in the mornings and she looks awful. I try not to notice or say any more than I have. I don't want her to worry unnecessarily. Why is it that when it comes to talking openly with the people we care about the most, at the most important times, we can't? Judgment replaces concern and we lose the opportunity to make a connection. We withdraw into business and the daily fare, waiting and watching the other to make a sign that it is okay to speak. And in that silence the worst imaginings seem confirmed. Are our worst fantasies worth the ache not confronting them brings?

I think of you and George. Can you tell him how bulldozed you feel when he stifles everything you say? He's a friend, isn't he? Isn't your friendship something you want to preserve? Sometimes it's worth the emotional work to make friends. George may not be able to admit he interrupts you all the time and filibusters to keep control, and you might have to hear from him some things that you won't like, but is this polite restraint better than the pain that ending it might bring? Don't worry so much about who's right or whether you're simply making it all up. Even if you are, that's part of the package and he needs to know that. Words are the gift of adulthood.

Am off in a few weeks to a conference center in North Carolina, one of those places where you relax on verandas and watch the trees grow. I'll call before I go.

I think I need to tell Peggy how much I love her. That would take care of *that* unfinished business.

Much love,
Mother

August 4

Dearest Amanda,

Well, here I am in a fine old fix: leg up on rickety stool, ankle swathed, toes looking like fat little sausages hanging off a bloated bluefish. Playing tennis, I rushed forward for a blooped serve and tripped over my soon-to-be-fat feet. The medical establishment in this heavenly hideaway insists that it is not broken, merely the worst sprain he's seen in decades. Well, that's comforting, although I need more reassurance than that when, after I soak it, the whole foot balloons up and resembles nothing more than a rubber glove filled with water to bursting. Got the picture? I think I'm incapacitated for a while.

I'm glad to hear that you and George are friends again. It sounds to me as if you did just the right thing. It isn't easy to have the kind of conversation that you described, where you both spit out your frustrations with each other, but it can't help but make it easier to resolve problems in the future. But hold on to your perspective. This George sounds like a persuasive and strong-minded character. And how many drinks after work does it take to settle the matter? I don't want to jump to conclusions (with this foot, it's a hop), but are you and George in danger of dragging out this fight just so you can resolve it over drinks and nurture the nice closeness that comes when you finally see that the other person doesn't hate you after all? In this case, maybe he thinks you're pretty special.

Beware the office romance. God, that sounds awful, but I'm afraid it's the best course. I know that after Tom, you must be feeling as if the only men you're going to meet are the ones at work and what the hell. But only under rare circumstances can it work out, and by that I mean both of you keeping your jobs and carrying on a successful romance at the same time. Oh, heaven, lying here, with my foot up, I think back and the pain of it still hits me hard, almost hard enough to take my mind off the awkwardness of this position. That position was even worse.

It was during that brief time of my life at Howard that I met Ed. He was the vice-president of manufacturing and I was the assistant to the vice-president of marketing. We would meet once a week in a matrix group formed out of representatives from marketing, manufacturing, design, and so forth. The matrix structure is great for some team development projects, but it can also be confusing. So we'd have more and more meetings to handle the snafus that we created after the last one.

Ed was handsome and athletic looking, but what attracted me most was his enormous energy and positive attitude. He thrived on challenges and as time went by I began to thrive on being with him. We'd stop for a while in the hall after our meetings and discuss what had gone on, then soon we were meeting for lunch, then drinks after work, then dinner.

When our friendly and tingle-filled chats turned into romance I'm not sure; who ever sees the first snowflake fall? For a while we were in a sort of snowstorm, sure that no one could see us or care about what we were doing. But we found otherwise. At one of the meetings, Ed had just proposed a design change that would make manufacturing a product much easier without altering the function one bit. It was a good suggestion, and I said so.

The guy from design leaned back in his chair and, twirling his pencil between his fingers, said, "That comes as no surprise."

All innocence, I said, "Why should it? It's a good idea and it doesn't affect the basic design."

"No," he answered, "but just let me try to get an idea past the two of you." He put his pencil down on the table and pushed back his chair. No one said a word. I didn't dare look at Ed; instead I looked at the others around the table. Not one of them would meet my eyes.

After that it was a quick sled ride to the bottom of a steep hill. I was iced out. If I'd been a secretary or someone without any power, I suppose it might have worked, or if Ed and I had not had to work together, but given that we did, others simply couldn't tolerate working with us. The backbiting and jealousy became more than either of us could stand and it put a terrible strain on our relationship. Ed's colleagues would shut up whenever I approached them in the hall, and I even received a few hate notes in the mail. I felt cut off and isolated from any support, and worst of all I think I began to doubt my own feelings. Not about Ed, although those were in question too by that point, but about whether I was a decent person or not. It's easy to accept others' views of ourselves.

Eventually it got so bad I had to leave Howard. Ed, nice as he was, wasn't about to quit his job for a romance that by then seemed pretty unstable, and if I had stayed I'd have always been the marked woman. It was a shitty deal, but that is the way the cards are still stacked.

What we would like to have happen and the present reality bear little resemblance to each other. We would all like organizations to be nurturing, supportive places, and someday they may be. This may be the great contribution that women can bring to work places. But you have to be realistic about today even while you work and hope that tomorrow can be different. And the present reality is that if you have an affair you may lose credibility at Crandall. People may see you as using sex to advance your career. Your contributions could be discounted and you could become suspect. Why women still receive the ancient stigma I don't know, but they do and will for a while, I'm afraid. The great danger is that you will begin to believe what others say about you. Women will always get it in the neck in cases like this, until there are so many of us that friendships and even romances between men and women become accepted realities. Maybe someday these powerful alliances will be welcomed for the benefits they bring, warmth and closeness, rather than derided for them. Women have a way of toppling the male order of things.

I hated business when I left Howard and I had acquired a bitterness about the corporate male that tarnished most of my thinking. Quite frankly, I never wanted to see the inside of a company again. It took me months to get what had happened into perspective. I had to accept that given the circumstances, everyone's response—mine included—made a terrible and human sort of sense.

Amanda, be sure of one thing. In order for you to go through what I know you will, be sure George is worth it. I don't think you can escape the consequences, not given the state of the corporate world today. You might be able to ride it out, the wave of abuse that will sweep you, but you'll be battered. And how on earth can you tell about George? It's like me being told I can put weight on my foot when it's strong enough to take it. A lot of help that is!

I sometimes wonder whatever happened to Ed. By the time I'd left, each of us had begun to believe what people said about the other, and it was too painful for either of us to find out if they were wrong.

Now I have to be off and soak the foot. Probably should soak my head at the same time. I can hear you now: "George? Oh, Mother, be serious." Love requires the perception of power reciprocated, opportunity, and need. And you, my sweet, have all three.

Much love,
Mother

August 14

Dearest Amanda,

I can't tell you how pleased and puffed up I was to get your flowers. I was sitting on the porch of the main guesthouse, grousing to myself while watching others gambol and frolic on the lawn like so many young ninnies. How silly, I thought, to expend all that energy on having fun when if they were smart they'd sit up here with me, legs raised, conserving strength for all the nasty thinking they have to do. Being a semi-cripple, I can see just how easy it is for the truly invalid to be quarrelsome and snappish. My voice becomes a little wheedling when I make requests, and a wheedle is only a croak away from a whine, a breath away from a bark. What on earth is there left to do? And then your flowers came and your letter, and I could talk normally again. Ah, the healing balm of affection. But is this ever a lesson in being powerless; if you don't have power in one area you create it in others.

When I think of that, it puts your story about the recalcitrant accountants in a different light. What was the problem? Every time you try to get figures from them on some prospects, they always have an excuse? (And earnings figures are no joke, I imagine.) And the more you push and try to set deadlines, the harder it is to get them to cough up the projections? And threats just make it worse? (You didn't say that, but I'm guessing.) When you described the problem, you made it seem as if it's an issue of time. My bet is it's not that the accountants don't have enough time but that they don't have enough power.

In most offices, an informal but real line exists between those who have power and those who don't. It may be the top few floors against the rest of the building. On the floors themselves, the dividing line is often down the middle of the hall or between one end of the hall and the other. At Howard, in our small department, the line was somewhere between the upstairs and the downstairs. Our department was housed in a separate building for a while, with all the thinking types, like me, on the ground floor and all the mechanical types, draftsmen, typists and our small press in the basement. Whenever I'd want some mechanicals done up or some reports typed, I'd have to make the descent. When the job was finished, you'd think, the person downstairs would bring it up. But it never worked out that way. The head typist would call me on the phone and very distinctly say, "This is Rita downstairs"—as if it were her whole name. "The report you want is done."

I didn't mind going up and down the stairs ten times a day—the exercise was good for me—but it began to bug me that Rita Downstairs refused to do the same. Not only did she refuse to climb the stairs, but when I'd go down with a rush job, she'd take it from my hand and put it on the bottom of her typing pile. We usually got things back when we needed them, but not always.

One day when I really needed to make sure that a report would get to me by early afternoon, instead of handing Rita the report I started rifling through her box to see what else was in it. Like a bear paw, her hand came crashing down on the box of papers. She didn't have to say a word; I withdrew my hand and handed her the report, saying meekly that I'd like it by two if possible. She nodded her head and as usual put the report under the pile that was already there. Something had to be done.

The next day I called Rita on the phone and asked her to meet me in the lunchroom. I went to the OK Corral with guns ready. Rita arrived after I did, walked into the lunchroom, where I was sitting at a table with a cup of coffee, and stood in the middle of the room.

"Well," she said, "what do you want?"

"Rita," I said, "I want to know how to get something to the top of your box if I need to."

"It's got nothing to do with me," she said. "You people upstairs have to figure that out."

"It's your box," I said.

"I just do them as they come."

"Do you ever change the order around?" I asked.

"Nope."

I was getting nowhere, and was about ready to give up the whole idea of rearranging Rita's box, when she said, "I'd like to."

"You'd like to do what?" I asked.

"Be able to change the order around, but I don't know what the order is besides the order they come in."

Thick, thick, thick. Because I had power to change my work schedule around, it had never occurred to me how little control Rita had over hers. In that situation we couldn't let her set the actual priorities, but we could let her know what our different demands were in a way that permitted her to arrange the work she handed out to the other typists. We solved the problem by meeting with Rita every Monday morning and going over the work that was likely to come in that week, giving her an approximate schedule of when we would need it. She then devised a wall chart on which she could track the different reports. She developed her own system of starring the rush items so that they wouldn't sit on other typists' desks. If I could have, I'd have moved her upstairs.

It's all very counterintuitive. In the face of powerlessness, you give power; you get it back tenfold.

Did you ever hear the story about the museum in Dublin that was left a treasure of art by a great collector? His family contested the legacy. One of their arguments was that the Irish didn't appreciate art, the proof being that they didn't have any. Well, Rita couldn't express power except in a negative way because she didn't have any. She didn't even have enough power to climb the stairs. . . .

Oh, guess who's here? Do you remember the summer you were in camp and were madly in love with Jim Jefferson? His mother and father are staying at the hotel, and they tell me that Jim is working in New York. He's a lawyer with some big firm, can't remember the name. He's just moved there and doesn't know many people. Why not give him a call? I know, "Oh, Mother," but why not? I told the Jeffersons you make the best beef Wellington. No, I didn't; just a joke. Now, if this isn't the ultimate in powerlessness, what is? So I'll take my own advice and get me some strength. Right now I think I'll try to walk down the stairs. "I think I can, I think I can." Ninety-nine thump.

Much love,
Mother

P.S. I was noticing the other day in the *WSJ* that the stock prices on Atlas are still low. Is the takeover going to plan? I'm so curious how you do these things. Would you mind giving your mother a mini-lesson in the art of acquiring a company. How do you know, for instance, what offer to make? Isn't Crandall trying to do an awful lot with this market on the rise?

October 5

Dearest Amanda,

I got your letter this morning. It hurt to read it, both because I have to accept some of the responsibility for what you're going through now and because your despair is so palpable and there's little I can do to relieve it. But I simply don't accept that certain "screw-ups," as you call them, happen because there's "something wrong" with you and whatever you touch will molder or tarnish. What could have given you the idea that every wrong turn of events in your relationships or at Crandall is your fault?

Did I somehow along the way give you the idea that you were lacking a basic quality that everyone else seemed to possess? It would be understandable, given how we lived, that you could have interpreted my absence and your father's disappearance as signs that we thought you weren't worth staying home for. But if this is so, can you imagine that you interpreted the signs incorrectly, that what we did or did not do had nothing to do with whether we loved you or not?

Others have their own motivations, which have little to do with us. Their actions do not reflect whether we're worthwhile or not. For instance, take the guy at the consulting firm you hired to do a financial audit of the Atlas acquisition prospect. You're so convinced that the initial meetings went poorly because you couldn't abide his picky questions. It may have worked out better if you had been able to, but if you accept all responsibility for the insufficient outcome, what do you learn about him?

I am convinced that women are particularly prone to define outcomes in terms of personal feelings of worth. When we do this in our private lives, we become self-absorbed and lose sight of the other person altogether. When we do it at work, where we need to see just as clearly, we lose the opportunity to gain valuable information about others. You need to know who is going to act positively about things you propose and who will fight them, and you need to know whether these characteristics belong to the people or to the situation they are in. You need to be able to judge the performance of your subordinates. And how can you do that unless you can see their actions as separate from your own (although with subordinates the line gets murky because they often dovetail their responses to fit)? It's so important to be able to see ourselves as separate from other people. Only when we do this can we see other people for what they are.

Why is being separate so hard, and why do we fight it so? It's called growing up, I guess, and why it's hard, for me at any rate, is that it involves self-esteem. It's an issue between parents and children—in this case, between you and me. Thinking we're not loved for what we are, we hang in there, fighting separateness, struggling to convince our parents that we're worth loving. If we convince them and "win the fight," then we can leave and be separate. But to leave and be separate before we've won the fight means living without self-esteem. But, dear one, it's a fight worth fighting *only*—and this is a very important *only*—if you read the signs correctly in the first place: only if I really did think you were not worth staying home for, only if I went to work because you weren't interesting enough to hold me at home, only if there really was "something wrong" with you. If you misinterpreted the signs, the fight is against foes that were never there, on a fictional battleground, for a prize that was always yours.

I grieve with you for the sadness, the disappointment, the many hours you spent by yourself. For these I am heartbroken; they are times with you I missed that are gone forever, and you are bearing the burden of them. If I could give you the days and hours back I would, but I can never repay you the time I owe. Never. And there is such great sorrow in that for me. But I'll never tell you I never loved you. If it's that fight you're looking for, that shadow war, don't look for me in the lists. I'm at home.

I love you,
Mother

Dearest Amanda,

I can't let the matter rest. There's too much at stake here. You are at a crucial time when you can use the great strengths you have to shuck off your old perceptions, or you can succumb to them. Try asking yourself the hard questions, like Copernicus, or like Kant, who, in the manner of Copernicus, asked whether all we see is as we see it or whether we color the world with the categories of our own minds.

Let's take specifics. Men. In your last letter to me, you wrote that part of the proof that there is something wrong with you is that you have such miserable luck with men. You cited Tom, the fact that Jim Jefferson turned out to be as handsome as ever but never called after your dinner party even though he said he would, and your colleague George Hertz, who, when you tried to talk to him about what might be happening between you, denied ever having harbored tender thoughts about you—as if seeing you in that light were unthinkable.

Now, we can take all these stories and examine them as impartial judges would. We can say we're impartial because we believe that to be the case. But even impartial judges are working on some sets of assumptions, otherwise they can't judge, right? Right. So here we are, you and I dressed in our black gowns and our white periwigs, sitting back listening to the cases for the defendants, Tom, Jim and George. Their esteemed spokesmen get up and all three make essentially the same kind of argument. Tom's lawyer says Tom rejected you because he found your needs too great, you demanded too much of him. Jim's lawyer says that Jim found your apartment too cluttered and your beef Wellington pastry a little puffy for his taste. George's lawyer contends that Amanda Hardy is a bit pushy, talks a bit too much, and tries too hard to "clear things up"—in other words, she's not subtle enough.

The defense rests and we the judges depart to our chamber to consider the evidence.

Now remember, we're sitting there with our set of assumptions. The world is flat, we say; the boats fall off when they cross the sea. And we believe that the sun moves around the earth, so that we are the center of the universe. We also hold dear to our hearts the belief that there really is something wrong with Amanda Hardy. How do we hear the evidence?

It all makes sense to us. We can just see that Amanda Hardy's demands on Tom would be too much. Given that there's something wrong with her, he was pretty broad-minded to tolerate her needs in the first place, and quite understandably he took off. And that acute Jim Jefferson needed only to look at that homey apartment and take one bite of that pastry to know that something was definitely amiss with Amanda. It was probably too cushy, that was it. And George, dear delectable George. He saw right through the scheming Amanda, the one who wants to get ahead and speak her piece. That Amanda takes things too seriously and can't see a little fun for what it is. Too dour, too uptight. The judges return and deliver the verdict. Guilty as charged, something *is* wrong with Amanda, and Tom, Jim and George get off scot-free.

But let us try the case with a different set of beliefs. Suppose we assume, silly us (but it might be fun to see the world upside down), that *nothing* is wrong with Amanda. Is it reasonable for Amanda to desire Tom not to sleep with other women, not to lie about it, and to make a commitment to her? Remember, this is after three years of being together regularly, years of good times and perceived reciprocity. Come on, Judge, what do you say? Ah, you say it is reasonable. I agree. What do we conclude? Maybe Tom has a problem with making commitments. Let's look at his record. Hmm. Interesting. He's over thirty and never been married, has not stayed in a job for more than two years, and buys one pack of cigarettes at a time.

On Jim the evidence is slim but, nonetheless, revealing. A handsome man, bright, and with good prospects. He gets asked to a dinner party by an old acquaintance in a town where he has few friends. Is it reasonable to assume that people want friends? Yes? Then it sounds as if Jim wants to be friendless. Or, and because we don't know, perhaps Jim left town for a while, or perhaps Jim is gay. Again assuming that nothing is wrong with Amanda, and that she is pretty and charming, Jim must be suspect. (This judge has inside knowledge, having recently met Jim's mother. She spent the whole time we were together describing Jim as if he were about to win the Kentucky Derby. If he hasn't developed a severe distaste for female appreciation of his looks, he's a better man than I am, Gunga Din.)

And finally we come to George, the great denier. Come on, Judge, give us an opinion. Who was it who arranged all those meetings in cocktail lounges after work? How much does George drink, anyway?

But here's an interesting question. If Amanda has nothing wrong with her, then by the same logic Tom, Jim and George have nothing wrong with them either. So what goes wrong? We act on our beliefs, our misconceptions, and view the world with misted eyes. Believing something is wrong with you, you may have clung to Tom too hard, admired Jim too much, talked too seriously with George. But those are corrigible malfunctions and quite minor in the ranking of interpersonal crimes.

To me the real issue is why don't we want to see the defects of others? Why do we fool ourselves into accepting responsibility for these painful relationships instead of seeing the reality for what it is? Perhaps the reality is that the relationship is unlikely to flourish, and that is a disappointment we don't want to bear. Associating disappointment with rejection with there being "something wrong" with us, we prefer to think we can fix the relationship, which means fixing ourselves. Ergo, something must be wrong.

So here, Amanda, from me to you is a piece of reality. Good men are hard to find ("good" means able to be intimate). This is true and always will be true. Men have it tougher than we do in this regard. Intimacy of the kind you seek can represent the first death throe to a man, the giving up of a long-sought-for independence from women. But if you can stop seeing their incapacities as reflections of yourself, you may find some wonderful people out there masquerading as "men." I have no proof of what I'm going to say next, it's only a hunch. Because men have a more difficult time making attachments than women do, my guess is that when they do, they make them at a more profound level. I suspect the world really is upside down and always was.

After these last two letters I've written, I'd love a chance to sit and talk. How would you like to meet me for a weekend in Bermuda? I have some business in New York on Friday morning the 24th and we could be on the beaches by four. I'll have Peggy make the reservations anyway and we can always cancel if it doesn't seem like a good idea to you. Okay? Here's hoping.

Much love,
Mother

November 12

Dearest Amanda,

Just a note to say I loved our time in Bermuda. It wasn't always easy, but it was good to talk with you. I'm glad you asked so many difficult questions about what I was like when you were growing up and about my relationship with your father. You have the most wonderful quality, you know. You're direct and don't shy away. I admire that so. Oh, I so admire you, Amanda, and sometimes I simply can't believe how lucky I am to have a daughter like you. And you looked so beautiful.

I've done a lot of checking for you and everyone here says Sanders & Company is perfectly fine for analyzing acquisition prospects but their strong points are service, not manufacturing, industries. Maybe you should get a second opinion.

Much love,
Mother

April 7

Dearest Amanda,

This is a postcard I found in an old handbag that I must have carried when I went to Italy in 1968 (!) and never sent. I found the bag in the cellar while I was looking for a file box. I send this to remind you that you may be only twenty-seven heartbeats away from the CEO's office now, but you were once small enough to swim in a tub.

Love,
mum

P.S. Do you remember what it was you wanted in red?

[Postcard]

Dearest Amanda,

You would love the beach I went on today. You would also love the ice cream and the hotel where I'm staying. It has bathtubs you can swim in and spaghetti for breakfast if you want—definitely Amanda country. Found what you wanted in Venice. Red too!

Love, *mum*

June 21

Dearest Amanda,

I don't know about you, but I'm hot. If this heat wave doesn't stop soon, I'm going to shave McMuffin. She walks around the house crying, lies down, gets up, lies down again. This morning I found her asleep by her water dish, her head half in the bowl, half out. I've taken to lying on the tile floor in the bathroom. Do you remember that awful summer it was so hot that we spent most of it sitting in a boat in dead calm, watching fish flop trying to get out of the hot water? Now, that's hot. Do you ever think of going back to Rhode Island to see those places again? I wonder if we'd recognize anybody at the beach or anybody would recognize us. How foolish! Of course they would; we were there for eight years, and I grew up there. But that seems ages ago.

101

Peggy is not reacting to the heat well at all. It really gets to her and although she tries to hide how tired she is, I know she's pulling on hidden caches of strength to get through the day. I am so worried about her, but she keeps telling me that she's fine. I'm afraid she's lying and that someday she won't come to work and I'll get a call from her sister saying Peggy's in the hospital. I try to give her opportunities to tell me, but the wretch is so damned proud that I'd be the last person she'd want to know if something really was wrong. Her whole life has been spent at Fairmont, a goodly portion of it working for me. It would probably finish her right off to stop working, so we play this silly game of let's pretend. All the while she's getting more bilious by the day and I try not to notice.

A good secretary is like gold, and if I lose her I'll be truly destitute at work, as well as having lost one of the oldest friends I have. It doesn't bear thinking about.

How are you getting along with Janet—any better? I'm afraid I don't buy the idea that the problem is that she's working for a woman. I've heard that women don't like working for other women, but I've never observed it to be the case. I know lots of women in business and all of them have female secretaries and the secretaries seem to work quite well. Besides, I have a natural bias against ascribing failures to a matter of sex. It's much more revealing to look at how the situations are being managed.

If you asked Peggy, and I will (in fact, why don't you call her yourself and ask her as well; she could probably give you some good pointers), she'd probably say that the things she hates most are contradictory expectations, namely, do this now but also do that first, which amounts to no direction at all, and negative expectations, namely, it's doubtful that you can do it right. And my God, when you're in a hurry it's so easy to deliver both. But I don't respond to either, so I don't see why anybody else should.

Remember me telling you about the guy I worked for here who proposed the interesting experiment by which we would ensure our control? Well, he had a few other annoying habits. One was giving me a project to do—say, figuring out a budget item—and then he'd check on me every few hours to see how I was coming along. Now, that's an empty statement on its own. It's not that he checked on me per se; it's how he did it. His attentions made it clear that he didn't think I would do the work or could without him. Ultimately I'd rush the bloody little jobs to get them out of the way, so I wouldn't have to deal with him. It's not his attention that was out of whack, it was his intention. As important as the occasional thank yous are interest and belief that the person can and will do the job.

I had a friend who worked for a bank, and every morning on his way to work he'd pick up a copy of the *Wall Street Journal*, a cup of café au lait and a croissant, and spend the first twenty minutes of the day going through the *WSJ.* One day we were having lunch and he seemed pretty dejected. I asked him what was wrong and he told me that he'd had a long talk with his boss that morning. It was his annual performance appraisal and apparently things had been discouraging. He had thought he was doing well and couldn't understand why his boss thought otherwise. Pressed for specifics, his boss informed him that he was lazy.

"Lazy?" my friend responded. "What do you mean, I'm lazy? I work hard from the moment I arrive at work to the moment I leave."

"No, you don't," his boss said. "You treat the office as if it were a French café. You sit there with your feet on the desk, reading the newspaper, munching on croissants."

I think it was the slam at the croissants that finally got to Bob, and within a year he'd left the bank for a better job at an insurance company. His boss is still at the bank, probably still losing good talented people because he doesn't treat them like adults. Just think of all the ways companies have of telling their employees that they are children not to be trusted, from time clocks to locked supply cabinets. For the few that abuse the system and the company's trust, managers cripple the rest of us. Who are the systems for, anyway?

Good question. Now I'm going to go take Peggy for lunch. Why don't you go out and buy yourself an air conditioner. I'll pay for it. It's too hot not to sleep.

Much love,
Mother

July 12

Dearest Amanda,

I keep thinking about what you said on the phone. Let me see if I've got it right. You feel in a slump, your commitment to your job is nil, and you feel about as motivated to work hard as McMuffin does to swim in the ocean. And you say it's not a question of belief but something else. You know you can do the work, you just don't want to, or rather part of you doesn't want to. You want to enough so you putter away at it, but you know a great portion of your heart and brain is snoozing on the sidelines. Believe it or not, this lassitude afflicts me as well at times, and I've never grasped where it comes from or why it disappears. Why, for instance, on this particular morning am I full of delight with the world and feeling ready to take on anything, while on others the attack is only a feint?

We know what we achieve if we're active and bound around like spring lambs, but what is our purpose when we limp around the pasture on three legs? I'm making the assumption here that none of our actions is meaningless, that even when we're not "doing something" we are in fact doing something. The law recognizes neglect as actionable; for instance, it sees passivity in the face of crime as complicity. So not doing something about our careers or our love lives has purpose in it. The question is what could that purpose be? What could be more important than getting on with the joyous business of creating and loving? I'm also making the assumption that working and loving take energy and that if we're not doing these things it's because our energy is directed elsewhere. We channel our strength and thrust down a side tributary while the main riverbed runs dry.

Remember talking about the great achiever in your office? Why is it he can get so much done while you spend the same hours gazing out of windows, doing enough to get by, but not what you know you could do? What is so distracting?

When we talked in Bermuda about your childhood and what I was like then, we really didn't talk much about what it was like for you. We speculated that you might have got the impression that your father and I didn't care about you because we left you alone so much of the time. But I wonder now whether something else got brewed during those afternoons you'd sit at home with Millie and watch television.

This may sound a little grandiose but, Amanda, did you get the idea that you couldn't do what I could do? I mean work and do well at it? I'm really reaching here, so forgive me, but who does the great achiever in your office remind you of? If it's me, then is it possible that what you're doing when you gaze out windows is not competing with me or not wanting to do what I did because you didn't like what I did. It did take me away from you, after all.

What would competing with me mean? That you might beat me, win, and be left alone? Amanda, I would never have left you alone if I didn't have to way back then, and if you became the chairman of Crandall tomorrow I wouldn't stop loving you. Please know this to be true. I would understand if you were angry at me a lot of the time, both for being away and for being something that seemed so unapproachable. But, dearest one, don't let the anger at all that define your purposes for you. If you hold back because of your ambivalence about work and competing with me, that's letting me define your purposes for you. What you want is what *you* want, and gazing out the window is not getting it for you.

I do my own share of hiding as well. I don't know why it comes over me still. Maybe it's a resentment bred out of a sense of not being loved, so that I had to go to work and support us. Probably part of me still feels that your father ought to have done more, or even further back that my mother and father ought to have been a nonstop cheering section. But they weren't and he didn't and I had to do it. So sometimes I hide, keeping myself from the good times. I play out a pattern whereby someone—not me—defines my purposes.

If you can see the situation as a choice between doing what *you* want and responding to an old bell, then it's easier to choose the happier path.

I mean, really, what does the great achiever have to do with anything you want to do anyway? He can't steal your thunder. The only way you lose the big bang is if you don't make it. Speaking of which, congratulations on the raise, very sizable indeed. No, I don't know much about Transmetal. I do know that one of our VPs who left years ago, when Gerald came, is there now. I think he's an exec VP now. I can check around and see what others know about him. In the meantime, let me know what you think of the above. Am I way off the mark?

> Much love,
> *Mother*

Dearest Amanda,

What a wonderful surprise to see you the other day! Peggy was so glad to see you, you know. She thinks of you as the child she never had and asks me about you all the time. After you left she said you looked wonderful, and you do. Of course, I think you could stand a few pounds on that frame. If you were going to model for *Vogue* I'd see the point. You barely ate a bite at lunch. I think you ingested more silver from the fork than you did food from your plate. How about if I made up a little care package for you: you know, chocolate-covered sparrows, grasshopper wings and ants. I think I'll include a teeny-weeny little silver fork to go with them in case you really want to gorge. Amanda, it's not *health*y to be so thin.

I loved your popping into my office like that and your parting comment: "Watch out, Ma, here I come." Girl of my dreams, you are welcome any old time.

I forgot to tell you while you were here what I found out about Stanley Sheldon. He was a very good detail man apparently, but not so great dealing on the outside. I think that was one of the reasons he didn't work out here after

Gerald arrived; Stanley just didn't do well in that kind of almost entrepreneurial environment, though I don't know what you envision for him at Transmetal. But go slow with these kinds of judgments; he may have changed a lot since then.

Did I say I loved seeing you? How I repeat myself.

Much love,
Mother

August 28

Matunuck, Rhode Island

Dearest Amanda,

Guess where I am? I suppose you can tell from the postmark, but what a wonder to be here after all these years. I got a call last week from Ruth White (I think you met her when we were here). I haven't seen her since then, but she was such a good friend. She told me that her father, who had been a close lifelong friend of my father's, had died and that in the midst of all the sadness and confusion she had wanted me to know. Ruth didn't ask me to come to the funeral and I was relieved because things at work are hectic as hell. After Ruth's call I resumed my frantic pace, but something gnawed at me. At first I tried to toss it off as a vestigial feeling of duty to your grandfather to attend the funeral of a close friend of his, and I balk at feelings like that as naturally as I have them. But the more the feelings intruded, the more I understood that it didn't have anything to do with my father and his life, but with me and mine.

Still ambivalent, I decided to go to the funeral. I thought it would be just a matter of flying to Providence, hiring a car, driving to the church, seeing Ruth, and leaving as quickly as I had come. But it didn't turn out that way. As soon as I entered the church and saw the people assembled there, I was absorbed into a community of feeling and shared experience that until that moment I had not realized had such a claim on me. "You can't go home again" because in some ways you never leave.

When Ruth saw me and I her, we both wept for the past as much as for the present, for our fathers and for ourselves. She asked me to drive with her to Matunuck after the funeral. She needed to come here to start sorting through her father's things, and although she didn't say so, I could tell she wanted the comfort of being with someone she didn't have to pretend for. And it turned out so did I.

So here, on the porch overlooking the pond where Ruth and I used to swim, I am, awash with belonging. If we resist the attachments we were given, we can never settle anywhere. And it's important to belong, Amanda; I worry about your keeping yourself so distant.

You know, as much as I might not want to have believed it at one time, if we're isolated it shows. When I think back to how I was when I first joined Fairmont, I shudder. Of course, life was one big hurt then, and I didn't want to get too close to anyone ever again. Also I thought that an impermeable facade would make it easier to bear the icy stares and cold shoulders of the men I first had to work with. In a sense it did; at least I didn't give the game away. But imperviousness carries a big burden with it; you do end up alone.

This has happened to so many men I know. Past a certain age, a lot of men don't have many friends, not in the way women do, at any rate. Their home lives are organized by their wives and their work lives by the politics of the organization. Unless they're lucky enough to live in the same town they grew up in, men as a rule don't have much opportunity to muck it in with other men. I can see the effects of this isolation from real friendships among many of the men I work with. It shows up in a sort of bluffness, and a tentativeness with others. (I've rarely heard men call their male friends from work to complain about the bad day they're having.) The terrible thing is that this cautiousness and arms'-length way of conducting relationships becomes the norm.

This is a long-winded way of cautioning you against adopting too much of the male stereotype. We pay for it. During my years of splendid aloofness, I had an assistant who was a wonderful person, and just married to a very nice guy who doted on her. After she'd been with us half a year she got pregnant, and then lost the baby in the fourth month. I think we sent her a plant or something innocuous like that. We took care of our obligations and concerns, organizational style. She came back to work and never mentioned the baby. So we never did either. Notice how I use the editorial *we* here; it's a nice way to spread responsibility. She left Fairmont within the year and as her immediate supervisor I had to give her her exit interview. She was leaving because she had got a better job, and really didn't have anything to say except that it had been difficult for her not having anyone at all say they were sorry about the loss of the baby. "No one, not even you." See why I shudder?

I worry, Amanda, that you might inadvertently be making the same kind of ever so natural and understandable identification with the "male" way of doing things. (Of course, there are exceptions, and enough of them, thank God, to have made some difference over the years.) I say this because outside of dear George, I don't think you've mentioned one person at Crandall in any context other than instrumental. I know I've preached about the treacheries of intimacy at work, but there is a middle ground on which you can stand. The trick is not to indulge in self-serving attachments where the aim is not reciprocity but a feathering of your own nest, whether it be emotional or organizational. Beware the attachments born out of greed and political maneuvering and nurture those where both of you enhance not only your own lives at work but also the organization. One of the things that women can bring to work is the courage to be soft and nurturant. As soon as your male peers see that the softness is not weak nor the nurturance smothering, they welcome these qualities. I don't know one text on good management that doesn't extol these virtues, except they usually call them human relations skills. Never let the chance to be supportive and engaging for positive ends pass you by. The saddest thing that could happen to organizations is women's burying their fine ability to form good robust attachments for fear they will be seen as weak. Of course, as I've said, some attachments are to be avoided, but these are generally with people you would have avoided in school, those you and Sylvia used to call "stuck-up" or the unlovely "grunts." George, it turns out, was a grunt, right? Or do I still not get it? Even if I never knew what you really meant by the term, you did. It still applies.

But I can't ramble on forever. The pond below is too beautiful and Ruth has suggested a swim. We will walk down the path, the dog running ahead, until we reach a spot where the brush has been cleared. Then we'll stand ankle deep in water on slippery rocks and push off into the satin surface. I know it will be that way; it was then. A week ago, I didn't know that this is something I know so deeply.

Much love,
Mother

September 10

Dearest Amanda,

Thanks for recommending *Chariots of Fire*. I rarely get to movies and this one was a real treat. Bill Rawlings was in town and we saw it together. He's Scottish on his mother's side and was really taken with the Highland scenes. I think I'm a little taken with him. Can you fly home on the nineteenth? I'm giving a cocktail party and then a bunch of us will be going out to dinner later. Bill will be here and I'd love you to meet him. Just for fun, of course.

Like many decent men, he doesn't believe the horror stories I've told him. Maybe you could tell them in a way I can't, with freshness. Men and women really do live in different worlds. Please come.

Much love,
Mother

P.S. I can't believe Peter Shell is being so difficult. He, Crane and the CEO *should* be involved in the acquisition program. It's a major strategy issue, not just a buying spree, isn't it? Our investment banker doesn't know one successful merger where the president and the CEO weren't involved. Tell Shell that!

September 26

Dearest Amanda,

What a rough row to hoe. Seeing Tom at a party with another woman sounds like the stuff of which nightmares are made. It's so much easier to get over a painful experience if you don't have to pretend you're having a wonderful time. So why pretend? Oh, I know at the party you didn't want to act like a mournful simp and go running out the door, like a woman on the cover of a love comic, tears waterfalling down your face. But why, now that it's over, take such an "I shouldn't mind" attitude? Of course you should mind. If it's painful, it's painful. I wonder where we got the idea that pain is something we shouldn't feel, that in some way it is unnatural?

114

And I don't see why you have to like her. I can understand the impulse to be pleasant and to refrain from scratching her eyes out—it tends to get blood on your dress—but why this need to be cozy?

I'm all for the great sisterhood of women, and think that we do have values that are important (and that business would do well to adopt), but to me something stinks in the Garden of Eden when we pretend to like people simply because they are women. Some women are not likable, and I don't see any more reason to like them just because they're women than I see reason not to like people just because they're men.

Who is that woman you work with who agrees with everything you say and then goes right ahead and does what she wants? Didn't she without telling you change a report you were writing together because she thought her way of phrasing things was more accurate? What she did showed the greatest contempt for you, but you bent over backward to be understanding and nice about it. But isn't there a "poor thing, she can't help it" factor in that attitude? Don't we stray awfully close to underwriting the female stereotype when we forgive each other for behavior that in a man we would revile? Aren't we in effect saying we *can't* help it?

What really bothers me about treating women in this special way is what it tells us regarding how we feel about women: It reveals a "secret sin." This is something I confess with dismay. I know that somewhere deep in my heart I still harbor the belief that men are superior. Everything in my experience tells me that women are just as bright and as capable as men (see how the comparison is set up!), but all that exquisite understanding isn't enough.

When I started out at work, pre–women's

liberation, having this feeling was normal. You were expected to have it. Even then I probably had less of it than most. I remember scandalizing a friend by looking for a job in the men's want-ads. Can you believe that just twenty years ago jobs were listed separately in the newspaper and no one thought it was odd? Fortunately for me, I was audacious, but it *required* audacity.

A year ago, I had lunch with Doug Blaisdell and a young woman who had just joined Fairmont, in Doug's department. The lunch was fine and we were all chatting along amicably when she turned to me and asked me where I'd bought my blouse. It was just the kind she was looking for. I answered her question and then quickly changed the subject. No one noticed, but I did. I knew the reason I'd changed the subject is that Carol had asked me a question that would show Doug that we were "just women."

Walking back to the office, I chastised myself mightily for this unseemly eruption from my subconscious. But later I realized that it is the chastisement as much as the assumption itself (that women are inferior) that creates the problem. Feeling guilty for a sociological reality lays the responsibility for it at my door. And it's not my fault. I didn't create the set of assumptions in the first place.

The real issue is feeling guilt about being a woman, and we have to catch it at every turn. But be understanding with yourself in this regard. We will continue for a while to make these slips, it's natural that we do. But the more we beat ourselves up about it, the more we tend to believe we aren't up to snuff and the pattern persists. And this may be the hardest of all. When I chided you for being soft on your coworker, was I beating you up a bit? It feels that way. Was I fearing that you're just a woman after all, like me?

How did I get here? Oh, yes, Tom and the woman at the party. How was he? Did you ever get that copy of *Hornblower* back from him? I'd like it if you did. I started reading the series again when I was in Matunuck with Ruth. They're much better reading than a lot of junk on the market and Horatio is such an endearing goof. I like him because he's a thinking risktaker (which should know no sex either). Better still, give it a read yourself. But start with *Mr. Midshipman*; you've got to meet him at his seasick, callow best.

Much love,
Mother

October 17

Dearest Amanda,

Good morning, sweet pea. It's so beautiful today and I'm feeling so very very fine. I can't think of a thing wrong with my life at the moment.

Saw Bill Rawlings last night. I guess I know what he sees in me—objectively, that is. I am so aware of all my faults. I can't cook very well, I'm not the slim jim I once was, I get unreasonably angry and scream (as if I were telling you anything you don't already know), I get depressed and grumpy, and at times my heart has a heavy beat. Dud dud dud. But he sees something else.

You know, I wonder if you're aware of how people at Crandall see you. You describe yourself as merely an efficient cog, but my guess is that you're seen as quite a bit more powerful than you think. If I had to pick out one thing that I've learned as a manager and as a human being over the years, it's that we can never ever (I usually don't allow myself to use those words) see ourselves as others do. Top managers especially lose all sight of how their subordinates see them. They forget how powerful they appear to people below them and how significant each of their insignificant actions is.

Our assumption usually is that we're less powerful than we are. At Howard, after I got my promotion I was the only woman who regularly attended the senior staff meetings. Remember this was in the ice age and women in top positions were an unevolved species. The senior vice-president would hold the meetings in the large conference room at the main building. We'd sit around the table and deliver our monthly reports on department progress. As he made his report, each man in the room would address his remarks to me. Instead of looking at the sr. VP, who was the highest-ranking person in the room, they'd look at me, the lowest. The first couple of times it happened I ignored it, but as it became a pattern, I found it confusing and disturbing.

I was so disconcerted by these glances that I tried to avoid them. I'd shift my eyes to the ceiling, to the wall, anywhere but at the speaker. I was conscious mainly that the speaker ought to be looking at the sr. VP and instead was looking at me. (It was like trying politely to steer off a man's advances while his sweetheart is watching.) Eventually I realized that no matter how evasive I was, the eyes still sought me out. So I gave in and looked back, nodding occasionally to show I was attending.

Here's the kicker. For years, literally years, I assumed that the men looked at me because I was the least threatening person in the room and therefore the safest person for their eyes to rest on. Now I believe that I was the most powerful person in the room. Not because of any hierarchical position I held but *because I was the stranger*, the person in front of whom they didn't know how to act. I was more threatening and because of that more powerful than anyone else.

So even if there are more of you women than there were when I was the object of awe, you're still seen as special and therefore threatening. Special? You bet. You must be "something" if you survived business school, got the kind of job you did, rose above the stereotypes, and can still smile. (You are smiling, aren't you?) Also, because you're a woman and everyone knows that the EEO is here to stay, it's more than likely that one of you is going to sneak through and really make it, and it might be you. So stop this "efficient cog" nonsense; it's important that you understand the true impact you're having.

Just yesterday, two unsuspecting women held up a mirror in which I saw myself as they see me. I was in the ladies' room on the floor below mine, one which I don't normally use. I was actually on the john and heard the outer door open. I heard two sets of steps enter the bathroom. The two women stood by the sinks, washing their hands and chatting away. They were talking about going to lunch and one of them mentioned that she would do some shopping, but didn't want to spend too much time at it. She had some appointment that she needed to get back for. Then they were silent for a moment and I thought it might be an appropriate time for me to make my presence known. I feel it's unfair to invade neutral territory without others being aware that one is present. Before I could give an "ahem" to announce my presence, one of them said:

"Margaret's on the prowl."

"I know. Steve said she was checking office space. Maybe she's bringing someone new in."

"No. That doesn't make sense," the first speaker said. "I'll bet she's checking offices to see if we're there."

"Oh, come on, that's paranoid. She doesn't care about you being at your desk, I swear. Check it out. Every time she's working something out she stalks the halls like a ghost." By then I decided the last thing I was going to do was let them know I was there. I was almost tempted to raise my feet above the door level. Instead I sat them out, amazed and horrified at the same time.

I'm not aware that I prowl. I also didn't know that people think I check to see if they are in their offices, or that I'd bring someone in without letting everyone know first. I wonder about the prowling. I guess I do get up and walk about a bit when I'm thinking hard about something. I get excited when my brain starts turning over, and the tension that creates sometimes propels me out of my office. I need diversion at these times to give me time to relax, so I walk down the hall looking for someone to talk to. It also is a time when I'll drop into someone's office to deliver something with a routing slip, which I've found is a great way to make myself available to people informally. When I walk down the halls checking offices, I'm seeing who doesn't look busy so that I can drop in without bothering them. Holy moly, the whole department has my every move deciphered and interpreted like an alien code. And I thought I was so obvious.

I don't think the gap between others' perceptions and your reality can ever be completely closed. All you can hope for is that the interpretations don't get completely outlandish. But there are things you can do, and more I should do.

I don't like to call unnecessary meetings—people are busy enough as it is—but I guess it's not a bad idea to have a few more debriefing times when people have a chance to sip from the same cup. I also think I'll prowl more often, not less. If people get used to seeing me hanging around, then my moves won't be so suspect. This will take time, but I can't think of a better way to spend it. My rule of thumb should be "Do whatever Gerald doesn't." I'd like to be the kind of boss I'd like to have.

Here is my new list of commandments:

1. When you're frustrated at something, don't put off dealing with it by picking on what your subordinates are doing.

2. When you see something you like, say so. Don't assume that people will assume the best. They usually assume the worst.

3. When you see something you don't like, also say so. People usually know when they're performing below par, and attention helps more than it hurts.

4. Don't shoot from the hip unless you mean to kill; subordinates can't always tell dummies from the real thing.

5. Pay attention to what others need to do their

jobs; in other words, keep the goodwill accounts full. If you have to make a withdrawal, it won't break the bank.

　　6.　Keep people informed of plans and events. What's trivial to you is sustenance for others.

　　7.　How you do something is often more important than what you do, assuming you know what you're doing.

　　8.　You can't be seen too often.

　　9.　You'll always be seen as more powerful than you feel, so walk carefully.

　　10.　Go to the bathroom more often.

Maybe someday I'll get it right.

Much love,
Mother

December 16

Dearest Amanda,

　　Oh, my dear, you sound so worn down. You must be exhausted with all this work, and I can truly understand your questioning whether it's all worth it. You work a twelve-hour day and go home to more work and an empty bed. I don't know what the rewards are myself sometimes; independence, for one, and I guess a sense of having done something well and solidly. But that's easy for me to say, I know. I have you. Regardless of what happens to my job or my life, there's you, a wonderful shining product that no one can ever deny. So, sweetest, believe me I can understand why when success seems a bleak reward, you think about having a baby. What a wonderful word it is, even. You say that you despair of ever finding a man you'd want to marry. It would be easy to find an intelligent partner who would have no responsibility besides a sexual one. And Sylvia seems so happy with her little boy. But, dearheart, what are you really looking for in a baby?

I remember when my mother died. It was before your father and I divorced, but he was away a lot and things were not great between us. Essentially I was alone. Except for you. On the day of the funeral, I came home and picked you up and hugged you, while I cried all the afternoon. I couldn't let you out of my sight. You even slept with me that night, and the next day I held on to you as if you were my mother and I were your child. I needed to belong to someone who cared for me, and my own mother was gone; there was only you. If I had been divorced then, it would have been you always, my sole constant source of comfort.

Amanda, the comfort I derived from you during those years might have been good for me, but it can't have been all that great for you. What a burden for a small child a single parent is. So from the child's point of view, it may not be the best thing.

And from yours? You are still the child you need to care for. I can't do it anymore except through my prayers and the occasional bossy letter, and my love, and my concern. The sense of need you have to belong you must fill from your own reservoirs of love for yourself. These must be full to the brim before you have a child on your own, and should be pretty near overflowing even when you have a husband to help.

123

A child is a wondrous thing, but it isn't something to have like a possession; it is something you nurture for *its* sake. All a parent can hope for is that the child takes over the nurturing process for itself, loving itself dearly as a prerequisite for loving others, especially children. And to me, Amanda, loving yourself dearly means not taking on too much when you're still so young and have so much still to garner for yourself. You are the person you should hug and comfort on the lonely nights until, because you are there, they aren't lonely anymore.

I love you,
Mom

P.S. Can't wait to see you Christmas. Have I got a surprise for you!

December 31

Dearest Amanda,

I'm all dressed up and waiting for Bill, who'll be here any moment. Just wanted to say it was lovely having you here for Christmas and to thank you again for the absolutely stunning blouse. I've got it on. It makes me look, well, positively full-bosomed. I'm wearing it with my long black velvet skirt. Look a little like a Good & Plenty.

What's the Shelley line: "If winter comes, can spring be far behind?" Well, on this dark night I'm sure it's true. Isn't it nice that the new year starts in the dead of winter, when the primitive in each of us deeply believes that we'll never see spring again. Right in midgloom, here comes the new year with all its hopefulness untarnished. Isn't it wonderful of it? I mean, who would care about the new year if it was in mid-July. It would get all confused with corn and elephant's eyes and no one would notice. They'd be too busy playing tennis and lying on the beach. Whoever planned it this way sure didn't live in Jamaica.

Happy New Year, darling girl.

Much love,
Mother

January 8

Dearest Amanda,

The news isn't good. I'm afraid Peggy's probably not going to make it. It happened just as I feared. Peggy didn't show up for work on Monday, and at about ten-thirty I got a call from her sister Helen, saying Peggy was in the hospital. Helen says the cancer is lymphoma and was always inoperable. Apparently it's just a matter of time—and not much. Helen wants to get Peggy home to Missouri so she can be with her mother, but I know Peggy wouldn't want that. If Peggy suspects for one moment what Helen has on her mind, I don't know what she'll do, but it worries me. I can't write more now, I'm too worried and am off to see Peggy in the hospital. I'll finish this later.

I'm back. And it's over. Peggy died this morning. I am shattered by the loss of her.

I was frightened badly during the last hospital visits, wondering whether I was doing or saying the right things. I was in awe of Peggy, who was facing something I couldn't see. But Peggy, bless her, made death a part of life.

At first she insisted on going through all the odds and ends at work so that I'd know where everything was. She made me take notes and joked about my dictation speed. Then when that was all settled, she leaned back on the pillow and just started to talk about her life, how she felt about it, what she wished for, and how it seemed to be just what she would have ordered if she had been given a menu on the day of her birth.

The next day we talked for hours. I was exhausted but she just kept going and I wouldn't leave her. At one point we played a game of gin rummy, but she couldn't concentrate very well. I was tempted to let her win anyway, but I wasn't about to cheat her of an honest loss. She'd never cheated me. Then toward noon, she seemed to lose interest in talking, as if her mind were focused on other things. She took hold of my hand and I held hers in the silence. I asked her if she could hear the birds, and she smiled. Then she said, "Thank you for pointing them out to me; I thought it was a steam kettle. I'm glad it's birds." And then she went away. Sometime in the next moment she just slipped into somewhere else and was gone.

And so here I am back at work and adrift. The emptiness of this office is huge. Peggy was such a touchstone for me. A corner of this Byzantine palace where

I knew I'd be safe. It's terribly difficult to make friends at work when you have resources at your disposal, like a question of whether you're being married for your money. But with Peggy the question never arose. We came through Fairmont together, and although we didn't share time outside of work, in this other life she was my best and trusted friend. I don't think I could have done it without her, and in the end she honored me with her trust. What a gift! I feel grown up, and so sad.

Much love,
Mother

February 4

Dearest Amanda,

See? Aren't you glad you decided not to have a baby by that big brawny brainy banker? Just think if when Tom called and asked you to dinner you'd arrived at Lion's Rock with a stomach already full. You know I never meant it wasn't a good idea ultimately. I can see having a baby if you have reached a certain age and the chances of marriage look slim and you have a good enough salary to afford all the help you'd need, but even then it would be so hard. All these things are relative, and you can quote me on that. And Tom? I'm so pleased for him that he's seeing a shrink. What a good sign it is. If he can successfully deal with some of those myths that haunt him, who knows?

The *WSJ* says that the stock prices on Atlas are still falling. What's happening to the takeover plan? Isn't Crandall's position in this becoming shaky? You sound a little pushed.

As for me, I'm still listening for the drumming of Peggy's fingers on my desk, still see her pass the door, waggling her hand at me as she goes. She's here everywhere. Oh, I miss her so!

When you see Tom again, send him my best. I got an invitation to Ginny's wedding. That was very sweet of her. Any ideas what she'd like? Am off. I'm breaking in Peggy's replacement. Her name is Barbara, and poor thing, she's heard from everyone how wonderful Peggy was and how close we were. What a handful to start with! I think I'll keep the lash hidden for a while. Probably a good idea, right?

Much love,
Mother

March 4

Dearest Amanda,

I didn't know that you are in charge of the Transmetal acquisition all on your own. I'm sure Peter Shell will want to check out what you've done before anything is finalized. That only makes sense. But even if he does, the responsibility for analyzing Transmetal appears to be yours. An occasion for celebration, no? Yet it's not surprising that you wake up in the middle of the night with sweaty palms. I can't begin to imagine the number of details you have to analyze and put into perspective on a deal like this, but I'm sure you can do it, Amanda. Other mortals do and most of them aren't as bright or resourceful as you. I understand your wanting to pull Crane into an active role, but seeing as that's not likely, isn't this a good chance to dispel the myth that you can't do it? We have to do it sometime. Giving up won't get you what you want in the long run.

Despite all the years I've spent in business, being on my own and making decisions, somewhere deep in the breast of me there still flutters a bird that wants to be taken care of. Don't be so hard on yourself, my love. Of course you want the easy way out on some days, and envy your women friends who are at home with babies and with loving husbands who pay the bills. I don't think there's a woman working who at some point hasn't been jealous of the wives of her male colleagues, as if they somehow had the better deal. And the lures to slip into the comfy roles are all around us.

But what are the rewards in always being unsure and afraid? To my mind, none. You know there's something perverse in all this. It's the same with stopping smoking or any other habit that we don't like. Women have a much tougher time giving up cigarettes than men do. Many of the men I've talked to say they gave it up simply because they got scared. At some point their dislike of fear became stronger than their desire for the cigarette. Women, or some of us, can go on being scared for a long time. It's

129

somehow easier to be afraid than it is to be responsible; as if being afraid were the same as being weaker and eligible for concern, as if being responsible were the same thing as being alone.

We sure got it upside down. But it's understandable that it will come back to haunt you, this primitive association we women are prone to. On those days, my advice is this: Ask yourself, "If I were not so afraid, would it be a good idea?" Feelings are just feelings; they don't always portray reality. The reality can be as you choose and want it to be. I've seen you do it. You can outlive the feeling. You did it the day you swam to the raft in the middle of Black Pond in Rhode Island. I'll never forget sitting there on the raft watching you swim, and the complete elation and victory that spread over your face as you climbed out of the water. "Mom," you said, "it's not the water that's scary; it's being afraid."

Some fears make sense and some don't, and it's important to know the difference. Is the cause of the fear the situation or your conception of yourself? Situational fear, like cigarettes or jumping off a cliff, make sense. Others rarely do. Telling the difference isn't always easy, and sometimes you have to hold your nose and jump in to find out. I still have to ask myself, If I weren't afraid, would it be fun or would I learn something from it? (Interesting. These are often things that many men do automatically, and can't understand why women hold back.) If I think it would not be a good idea or is at least questionable, I wait until I see how I feel about it on more than one day. When you can tell the difference, you can afford to take the risks at work and bear the burdens of success. By that I mean seeing responsibility as something different from isolation, achievement as liberation rather than abandonment.

Oh, my, what a trial life can be at times; all that success and nothing to wear.

Much love,
Mother

P.S. You never said what you wanted for your birthday. So I'm going to make you a surprise ball—remember those from your birthday parties? Well, just you wait till you see the surprise ball to end all surprise balls!!!

April 19

Dearest Amanda,

So that's it. You've been so secretive lately I didn't know whether you were planning a palace revolution or a simple trip to outer space. It had crossed my mind that you might really be a spy and Crandall just a clever cover story. Are you sure you're really not a spy at the same time the business media have you pegged as the smartest thing to hit the acquisition area in years? What a coup taking over Bufford-Walters would be. Talk about diversification! What do you do with a major electronics company if you get it? And what about Atlas? Isn't this all happening rather fast?

As I've said before, the ins and outs of these things fascinate me. If everything works out, how long before you know whether you'll keep the old management? Or do you figure that all out ahead of time? I assume the latter, partly, but aren't there some tired old birds there who still know what they're doing and can contribute to the company still? I guess I have a warm place in my heart for old buzzards, being one myself.

I suppose all the top people at B-W will have platinum parachutes and the bail-outs will be considerable, but I hope not. Oh, it's easy to see why senior executives flee when a takeover occurs, but in a sense it's the height of immorality to do so. It makes the company into nothing more than a collection of pension plans and stock options, as if the people working for the company, the stockholders and the trusting customers don't stand for anything. These people take so much with them that can't be replaced by simple professional management.

You know, when Gerald became CEO of Fairmont, it was after a pretty slack period. Growth had slowed a lot and momentum was scattered like mercury bubbles. All this had happened, I thought, because we'd got ourselves unfocused from our original line of business and were making excursions into all sorts of areas we didn't know beans about. Marketing tools is a hell of a different trick than marketing leisure-time equipment. So we were at sixes and sevens, but there were masses of good people here. Anyway, the board panicked and brought in Saint Gerald, who would slay the dragons of inefficiency and no growth. Have you ever actually met Gerald? He's not very prepossessing. When I first met him, I thought that with a head that size he was bound to be brilliant, and that his dour demeanor promised serious action. He was given the

132

usual honeymoon period, during which we all watched and waited to see what he'd do. I was wrong.

The first thing he did was to call the most senior of us into his office for a get-to-know-each-other chat. We each had half an hour on his schedule. When I walked in, Gerald was sitting behind his desk. He half stood, and motioned to the chair that faced the desk, so that I would be sitting opposite him. There were a couch and chairs and a coffee table in one corner of the office, but we were clearly at the business end of the room. As soon as I had sat down, Gerald also sat. He took off his watch and leaned it against the pen and pencil set at the head of his desk blotter. He then sat back in his chair, made a steeple out of his fingers and, resting his chin on the tips (he'd seen too many movies), he asked me what I did. I started to explain what I saw my function as being, but before I could get more than few sentences out, he leaned forward and said:

"What do you think of Doug Blaisdell?"

I told him I thought Doug was one of the most gifted and sensitive executives I knew. Tops.

"What about Dan Hupert?"

As I opened my mouth to speak, he took out a pad, lifted his pen and looked at me expectantly. It was a rat session and the biggest rat of them all was in the room with me. I gave only cursory answers from then on, finally explaining that I thought each person could speak for himself far better than I.

Gerald picked up his watch, strapped it around his wrist, and thanked me for my time. How well did he know me? Or anyone?

I didn't see Gerald again to speak to in any informal way for at least four months. By that time, five senior vice-presidents, a group manager and an executive vice-president were missing from the ranks, presumed dead. Also gone were some old-timers who had peopled the halls like family pets. One of them, Eddie DeMeo, had worked in manufacturing for thirty-five years. If you found a stray bolt on the factory floor, Eddie would know the machine it had come from and why it had fallen out. Keeping track of bolts was not Eddie's job, he was in line scheduling, but he just loved the machines and everyone knew that Eddie knew more about how they worked than the people who ran them. Eddie's function wasn't official, though, and when Gerald, looking for ways to cut corners, cut off a few heads, Eddie's was one of them.

The moral to the story is not neat. The machines didn't all spring their bolts the day Eddie left. In fact, the equipment worked just fine. But something more important disappeared. He kept things together down there by caring about the machines. When he was gone, people didn't feel so sure anymore about why it was so important to keep things nifty. Eddie was also a great talker. He'd tell you just how a line was working or what he thought might be wrong with a product design. He wasn't telling tales; he'd just mention it in passing because it seemed important to him. When he left, some information just stopped getting passed around. And Saint Gerald, in his timed encounters with the world, had never even met Eddie DeMeo.

It takes a long time to know what makes a company run. Have you read *Corporate Cultures* or *In Search of Excellence?* Despite some flaws, both books point to the things I'm concerned about. But neither gives much notice of what is to my mind a serious, maybe *the* serious, management problem. I don't even know what to call it, something like responsible citizenship. My experience is that most people simply don't look beyond their own purviews. They are content with doing what is on their desks, eating what is on their plates, and looking out the same windows day after day. I suspect there is a measure of security to be gained from limited routines, but it means that in every organization many eyes are blind. Many people want sharply defined job responsibilities so that they won't get caught outside them, doing something wrong. This attitude would be fine if organizations were neat little boxes, but they aren't; even the ones that look that way on charts aren't. An organization is as large or as small as the actions of the people that form it. Your job, for instance, because it will affect the lives of so many people, has an immense scope. You may not be the CEO of Crandall or of any of the companies you acquire, but because you know about them and have impact on them, they are your responsibility in the sense I mean. I wish I knew more about why so many people flee what they see needs doing. Why is the line "It ain't my job, man" a joke instead of an indictment? I suspect we all feel leaderless and will be damned if we will do the leader's job. But that is so primitive and childlike, and if we're going to be anything in this world, we might as well be adults and, in recognizing that our actions have impact, take responsibility beyond our immediate interests. Besides, if we don't, few will, and then we get people like Eddie DeMeo losing his job because no one who knew better spoke up. Me included.

I haven't thought about Eddie in a long time. I still miss him. I wonder about myself and how long I should stay here. I have been here so long and I can't imagine working anywhere else. But I know I could and it would probably be good for me. It's hard to give up old ways, Lord knows.

One offer has been made recently. A new kind of job altogether. Bill Rawlings has asked me to marry him. I find that hard to imagine too. (Not that he's proposed; I've gotten used to that during the last two weeks—it happens daily.) It's the idea of changing, getting on with it, one more time. I'm so settled here. "Maybe too settled?" she asked weakly.

Isn't there a Ted Hughes poem about a hawk surveying its world, which creation fashioned to suit it, and saying, "I am going to keep things like this"? As if one had control, as if this old buzzard could fight change.

Much love,
Mother

P.S. What do you think?

April 28

Dearest Amanda,

I was having lunch today with Albert Epping—he's on the Makepiece board with me—and he said that he'd heard from someone he sits on another board with that the

Bufford-Walters deal may not be the picnic it was once thought to be. Has something happened? Is there a way you can back out if you need to without too much loss? If you want me to find out more from Epping, I will, though I suspect every word and letter of this is old news and I'm bringing you last year's headlines. Fat lot of use I am.

. . . I'm glad you called just now, but I want to repeat what I said on the phone. What is the worst that can happen? The B-W deal goes through and something is found after the fact. That's possible, it could happen. But don't prepare for the worst. All I can suggest is that you go back to your numbers and check them again and again, not because you'll find the error you're looking for but because you probably won't. Ever had that feeling that you've left the gas on in your apartment and then you spend the next four hours worrying and fretting? Well, it's so natural with me that I routinely go back and check. I know it's absurd and I've yet to find the gas on, but checking makes it possible to have a good time. And, dearest, this is my main concern. You've been working so hard that you've given yourself zero time to enjoy yourself. What does Tom think? Would it be possible for just the two of you to get away for a weekend or something? Or come here, and Millie will serve you tomato soup and saltines on a tray in the sunroom and you can watch soaps. Whatever, get away from it.

Now for my news. I meant to tell you on the telephone, but we got so swept up in the B-W maze. I've decided to marry Bill. Just writing the words gives me great pleasure. At the same time, I am so conscious of the pain of letting go of so much that has seemed to be me—the house, Millie, Fairmont. But then when I think of Bill and how extraordinarily good he is to me, all my reservations are canceled. Somehow in his quiet persistent nonflamboyant way, he has managed to fill all the hidden crannies of my heart. I love him very much.

We're planning on being married August 21, but will change dates if either you or Bill's children, Cynthia and Bruce (you'll like them a lot), can't make it. We want to give you enough time to arrange schedules. I'll stay at Fairmont through July and then we'll have time to sell the house and start packing before the wedding. I suspect we'll be spending most of August in San Francisco, house-hunting, and I'll be talking to a few companies in the area. I've already been called by a few, so I have no fears about finding a new job. Probably in a computer company of some sort. God, can you imagine, me and computers! I am excited about the possibilities, terrified of the newness, but it all makes a huge amount of sense to me.

How Bill is going to put up with me, I don't know. He insists that I could just sit dumb for the rest of my days and he'd adore me, but that's just courtship talk. He wouldn't adore the wreck I'd become; besides, he knows very well that I couldn't do nothing.

I know you have tons on your mind right now, but if you have a chance I'd love to hear what you think. It is important to me, you know. At one time I had thought that if I ever got married again, I'd write your father a small delicate note. Now I see it would be irrelevant, a leftover.

Please don't worry about B-W too much, and do something to give yourself a rest. Are you getting enough exercise? That's important. Let me know how you are, *please*.

Much love,
Mother

P.S. This may sound silly and I feel silly asking. But is it all right for me to stay at Bill's before we get married? Now I ask you, isn't that dumb? Some habits die hard.

June 7

Dearest Amanda,

When you called this morning you sounded so beaten. I wish I could have said more on the phone to make you feel better; I know you're feeling terrible that the Bufford-Walters deal has turned out so badly. It is a big blow that after the fact you find deadly pockets of rot in the form of promised orders B-W can't meet as well as bad product development on a crucial investment. Yup, all these things appear to be true, and it is also true that you might have found out about them if you'd dug a little deeper. Okay, let's get the cards out on the table. Were you so anxious to pull it off you skimmed the cream without smelling the milk at the bottom of the bottle? Is this all your fault?

For starters, you might begin by recognizing that while preparing the Bufford-Walters reports you were responding in part to the pressure Crandall was putting on you. Right? If I remember correctly, you weren't given much time to go over all the possibilities—Atlas, Bufford-Walters and the other companies you were considering. A pushy management can force employees to make decisions faster than they might, given their own choice. So doesn't Crandall have to bear some of the responsibility here? Also, it's never been known as an acquiring company, so my bet is that no one there really knew what to do and that you and Peter Shell were working somewhat in the dark. Yes? Okay, so in the dark you don't always see clearly.

For the sake of being fair, then, let's say at least 50 percent of the responsibility belongs to Crandall and 50 percent to you. Now, what's the worst we can say about you? That you wanted to succeed too much. Why? Who are you trying to please? Because it sure sounds as if you weren't pleasing yourself. Me? Would it please me to have you push yourself to the brink of exhaustion just so you could pull off a coup? Not much, it wouldn't. Just the reverse. So what happened? My guess is that your biggest failure is not trusting your own judgment and so you came up with an opinion before you were ready. But my God, Amanda, think what you know *now* about trusting yourself. I hate to say this, but out there you really are alone and you have no better friend than yourself. I can't tell you to feel better and have it mean anything unless you know that the only mistake you made was not to listen to yourself carefully enough. And that you can do better now. I'd take your advice, freely given, any day.

But I realize this probably doesn't help much when you're struggling with disappointment and how to face your co-workers. Amanda, can you accept that you're not perfect? Remember my writing you about the day Sheba died and my feeling that I was somehow at fault? I didn't want to recognize her death or mourn her openly because it seemed that implicit in that was acceptance of my own failure. The grieving meant that I was wrong. But I couldn't feel better until I accepted her death on her terms and felt her loss as something that had happened outside me, until I had—not forgiven myself (because that implies culpability)—accepted that there was no question of my being in control, of being to blame. She was gone, and all my hanging on to blame and self-recrimination wasn't going to bring her back.

Isn't it the same for you now? If you blame yourself, doesn't that still connect you to the events, as if in some magical way, by beating yourself hard enough, you could change them? It has happened and you must let go of your control of the events. The disappointment is real, but the facts you cannot change. And, sweetest, your colleagues are not the problem. As soon as you begin to feel freed of blame, you will act more confidently and they will treat you as you treat yourself. I understand your instinct to run away and your thinking about a new career and I can't advise you what to do ultimately. What seems important to me, however, is to wait and not to act while you're feeling so angry with yourself. Give yourself time to acknowledge the disappointment for what it is—not an indictment, but a loss.

Be gentle with yourself, for your sake.

Much love,
Mother

Dearest Amanda,

The last month must have been hell for you. A vacation right now is a splendid idea. So much the better if Tom can join you for part of it. I hope he can and that you will let him help bind your wounds.

You are so much more than just these wounds, my sweet. They may be all you can feel right now, but they will stop hurting eventually. In a way, it's as if you've given birth to yourself and have the experiences of your own life to mend you. You can be a far better mother to yourself now than I can. Listen to yourself carefully, for you know so much now that is worth hearing. You know how to work and how to have fun, how to love someone who is not perfect, and how to forgive us, who love you so dearly, for not being so.

I'll probably not be writing quite so often for a while. I'll be up to my ears in the little and the great, saying goodbye, doing a lot of mourning on leaving Fairmont, and rejoicing with Bill. But, my dearest, I'll be thinking of you always, loving you so much, no matter where I am, no matter where you are or what you decide to do, forever.

I feel a little odd right now, going away and so much going on in your life—or is it the other way around?

Could you come home before the twenty-first, perhaps? Look who's having a hard time letting go. And you thought you were the one who needed all these letters. I've always felt your hand in mine. Thanks.

I love you,
Mother

ACKNOWLEDGMENT

I owe much to my friends: Harriet Rubin, my editor at Harper & Row, who always saw more than I did and gave me the guidance to see it as well; Shoshana Zuboff and Nan Stone, who read the manuscript at critical stages and helped me to shift courses; Alan Kantrow, for lending me Lorimer; and above all, Maureen Baldwin, whose encouragement and desire to read more was my daily bread.